HIDDEN
—IN—
PLAIN SIGHT

REALIZING THE FULL POTENTIAL OF
MIDDLE LEADERS

MICHAEL R. IANNINI

© 2019 Michael R. Iannini
All rights reserved.

No part of this publication may be reproduced, distributed, or transmitted in any form or by any means, including photocopying, recording, or other electronic or mechanical methods, without the prior written permission of the author, except in the case of brief quotations embodied in reviews that include full citations, and certain other noncommercial uses permitted by copyright law.

ISBN: 978-1-7340583-0-7

eBook ISBN: 978-1-7340583-1-4

EDU032000 EDUCATION / Leadership

EDU050000 EDUCATION / Collaborative & Team Teaching

Edited by Rochelle Deans and Sydnee Hyer
Cover design by Angela Baxter

For orders, additional resources, or inquiries, please visit
www.middleleader.com

PRAISE FOR *HIDDEN IN PLAIN SIGHT*

Michael Iannini's "Hidden in Plain Sight" is a comprehensive and explicit acknowledgement of the essential role that middle leaders throughout organisations have as change agents. The book is brimming with stories that leaders can identify with and practical tactics that they can then adopt. In my experience, the degree of impact of a school or organisation is directly proportional to the ownership and engagement of middle leaders in the 'engine room' who are focused on converting the school stated strategy into action. Michael's book will equip and inspire leaders as they learn the art of transformational collaboration.

DR CHRIS JANSEN – LEADERSHIP LAB, UNIVERSITY OF CANTERBURY, NEW ZEALAND

In this book, Michael Iannini uses lessons learned from his years of experience in international education, helping schools such as Shanghai American School to achieve their goals. Building capacity within an organization is one of the key levers to effect change and Michael proposes concrete strategies for senior leaders and middle leaders alike to create that capacity. Readers will appreciate the big picture framework provided by the first six chapters as well as the practical tools developed in the last five, that can serve as a great book study for leaders and teams. While there is a lot of research on teacher leadership and middle leadership, the context of international schools is often poorly understood, and Michael Iannini contributes to filling a gap in an area of key strategic importance. I am thankful to Michael for putting on paper theories and practical applications our teachers and leaders were only able to access so far through workshops and professional development activities.

DR. EMMANUEL BONIN | CHIEF ACADEMIC OFFICER - DEPUTY HEAD OF SCHOOL, SHANGHAI AMERICAN SCHOOL

"Hidden in Plain Sight" brings a new, and long overdue, perspective on how schools can assess and modify their organisational structures and practices to put deputies, teacher leaders and coordinators at the centre of transformational change. Meaningful change across a school requires a great amount of energy and collaboration. It is great to see many of the ideas and beliefs I share with Michael about the role collaboration plays in improving student learning captured in this book.

RAMI MADANI, HEAD OF SCHOOL, THE INTERNATIONAL SCHOOL OF KUALA LUMPUR

One of the most used but least understood buzzwords in education is collaboration. Michael Iannini's new book 'Hidden in Plain Sight: Realizing the Full Potential of Middle Leaders' looks at the critical role middle leaders play in schools. Regardless of school structure or the titles educators are given teacher leaders have the potential to bring educators together through genuine collaboration. This book offers practical, research-based ideas to leverage the inner leader in us all. There's a simple message that suggests well-planned empowering teamwork, through use of collaboration techniques, can lead to positive, sometimes transformative outcomes. Having worked with Michael Iannini and witnessed his high-quality approach to delivering professional learning through PD Academia he is definitely someone who walks his talk.

LAURIE MCLELLAN - DIRECTOR, NANJING INTERNATIONAL SCHOOL (FORMER BOARD CHAIR AT ACAMIS)

—TABLE OF CONTENTS—

FOREWORD — vii
PREFACE — 1

SECTION 1: BUILDING THE FOUNDATION — 7
CHAPTER 1: Who Should Lead? — 9
CHAPTER 2: Where Middle Leaders Thrive: Seeding the Culture — 18
CHAPTER 3: The Silo Dilemma — 27
CHAPTER 4: Outputs vs Outcomes — 36
CHAPTER 5: The Sandbox — 49
CHAPTER 6: Building Middle Leadership Capacity — 61

SECTION 2: LEADING EFFECTIVE TEAMS — 79
CHAPTER 7: Team Formation — 81
CHAPTER 8: Workshop 1: Building Trust — 94
CHAPTER 9: Establishing Purpose — 107
CHAPTER 10: Facilitating Purposeful Meetings — 122
CHAPTER 11: Collaborative Communication — 136

FINAL THOUGHTS — 152
BIOGRAPHY — 156

————FOREWORD————

About eight years ago, Jim Koerschen, or Dr. K as we fondly referred to him, and I had one of our monthly meetings as Heads of neighboring international schools to discuss the complexities of leading and developing international schools in the rapidly and ever-changing environment of emerging China. Jim and I had become close friends not only through our Christian beliefs, but having had the good fortune to spend half our careers in universities and then transition to international schools. We relished those times for discussion (and venting), for we both faced similar macro-development issues in different parts of Shanghai, he in Pudong and I in Puxi where local education bureaus would often interpret education policy differently, resulting in contradictory outcomes for similar schools. Such complexities occupied enormous amounts of time, political awareness, cultural sensitivity and ability to explain to the public what was often not understandable or easily explainable.

We also served together in two professional organizations in China, the first was Shanghai International Schools Association (SISA) and later the Association of China and Mongolia International Schools (ACAMIS). Knowing that other Heads across China who were members of ACAMIS faced similar problems, we contemplated how they could perform their different, demanding roles and still meet the expectations of a leader that bright and mobile parents and teachers brought with them from previous experiences in other countries. We concluded that we were fortunate to have gained valuable insights from our university experiences that could ultimately have a human impact that makes a difference such as: in independent education we have an

FOREWORD

opportunity, if not obligation, to create distinctive models of international education; with the high degree of transience among parents and teachers in developing countries, every opportunity to greet or meet someone is precious and should be treated as special; we realized from our interactions that we benefitted from experiencing highly collegial and congenial working environments in university; to create special learning models, we needed a steady flow of highly motivated teachers and leaders who could adapt quickly to a different culture, both within the host country and within the school...special people who look as these opportunities not as a job, but as a way of life and also commit to the unique philosophies of each school that guide the creation of the model; and that such special people need ongoing professional development and a voice in the development of the school.

This was fun stuff and a great deal of our interactions with others was reinforced through these monthly meetings. We knew that with all the diversions we experienced from the normal responsibilities of a Head of School, we needed to rely on middle management roles and develop a group of leaders who were prepared to make the same commitment to creating unique models that we made. But as many of the experienced leaders, no matter what the specific role, came from state education in different countries, our greatest concern was to avoid establishing authority realms that were guided by a 200-page policy manual. We had to find a way to train or retrain middle managers to think first about the philosophy of the school and then creatively bring the philosophy to life, to be good listeners and ask questions in order to understand concerns that are raised in the various constituencies, to allow teachers to have a voice, to set goals and seek input from many sources as to how to attain them, to encourage student input on relevant issues and to explore ways that students could be given responsibility and become independent thinkers and learners so they can better shape their futures. Most of all, while we valued experience, we prized those who, rather than providing all the answers, knew how to engage others to build teams and teamwork in order to have as many people part of and contributing to solutions as possible which not only utilized the insights of others, but it also contributed to their own growth as aspiring leaders.

FOREWORD

As we each set about trying to accomplish those initiatives in our own schools, we also contemplated how this might be done in a larger forum to assist other international schools with their development. ACAMIS provided an incredible opportunity to do this. We were both elected to the ACAMIS Board of Directors and two years earlier the ACAMIS Board had authorized the idea of a Middle Management Conference that attracted about 100 participants from the 48 ACAMIS member schools at that time and a prominent workshop leader was contracted from abroad to lead the conference. About a week before the event, the speaker indicated he could not come and the conference had to be cancelled. Naturally, the Board was reluctant to try that again. Two years later, during one of our "what do we need and how can we provide it" discussions, we realized the negative hangover from having cancelled an event for aspiring leaders, but felt we needed to try again. Instead of thinking bigger, we decided to start small. Instead of inviting anyone who wanted to come, we set a limit on the number of participants and were determined to create a special interactive environment where participants could interact, question, share, discover, inspire and be inspired. Neither of us had time to develop the idea or the content so we began the same way we worked to build great schools, seeking someone with special personal qualities and experience who could facilitate rather than lecture, relate to and utilize examples from the everyday realities of participants rather than textbook theory and who could define skill sets from participants' experiences while providing an inspirational, encouraging and fun workshop environment.

As we did in selecting our own leadership teams, we chose to seek an articulate, dynamic, highly-motivated, confident individual with an outgoing personality and strong personal qualities who could create a special workshop environment and make things happen. After relating our set of criteria to candidates, we easily agreed that Michael Iannini had the qualities and ideas we were looking for and we were not disappointed. From the resurrection of the Middle Management Workshop that remains one of our most popular ACAMIS workshops, Michael has developed over thirty different types of workshops in eight years that he rotates from year to year in helping us to define and meet the needs of our members. Eight years later, also learning from those in his workshops, he has become the

FOREWORD

kind of independent, creative-thinking, inspiring leader we hope he shapes for us in our schools to lead from the middle and has put his experiences into print to keep us moving in that direction.

Tom Ulmet
Executive Director, The Association of China and Mongolia International Schools (ACAMIS)

PREFACE

Several common frustrations dominate discussions regarding leadership in almost every school I consult, whether working with the board or training front-line administrative staff: (1) the concept of "us versus them" and (2) there never being enough time to do what is being asked of staff. In my experience, an underlying tension always seems to simmer between non-academic and academic staff, as well as between teachers and the various layers of leadership in a school. These tensions often surface as a result of the second problem, time, and, more to the point, how time influences relationships across the school. This problem of time is the result of the myriad initiatives that senior leaders and other governing bodies try to force through at the start of the school year based on the premise that they only have 9 months to get everything done. Everyone is excited at the start of a new school year, but within months, most can't wait for the school year to end.

As I delved into the roots of these problems, which grew very deep, I found several organizational obstacles that were common across all schools. Many of these obstacles had a type of folklore to them, in that regardless of how schools tried to innovate and change, they always did it within an unchanging box. This box was built decades ago and was defined by how schools did budgeting, calendaring, strategic planning, recruitment, and admissions. This proverbial box suffocates the desire for change, as it provides very little incentive for the most important change agents, the middle leaders—the teacher leaders, coordinators, department heads, and vice-principals.

The problem of time is more pronounced with middle leaders wearing multiple hats, including the hat of a classroom teacher. Some middle leaders are not in the classroom, but are still hindered by the time problem, and it is most likely because they are too invested in the work of the teams they supervise and involved in too many initiatives. The time dilemma doesn't solve itself, regardless of the number of tools and techniques we use. What does help to alleviate the time dilemma is when middle leaders are thoughtfully selected, supported and bought into the initiatives they are asked to achieve. Senior leaders (principals, heads of school, superintendents, and board members) must also acknowledge that leadership isn't just something someone does, but rather something that requires careful planning and coordination.

This book is for middle leaders in schools, from those brave enough to volunteer to lead a grade level or subject team, to those pursuing advancement in their career. Whether you have just accepted a leadership role or have been leading teams for many years, this book will provide guidance on how you can foster greater interdependency among team members and develop a sustainable collaborative team culture.

Senior leaders will benefit from this book by the provided insight into recruitment and professional development (PD [1]) strategies for middle leaders. The primary objective is to develop (or increase) knowledge, management skills, and confidence for middle leaders, who are relied upon to be change agents in schools. A secondary objective is to challenge the beliefs and practices of senior leaders that can limit the potential and growth of middle leaders.

This book is not just a culmination of everything which I have experienced, learned, and implemented, but rather the collective experience of every middle leader and senior leader that has desired to achieve some level of change—if not in their school, then in the way their team collaborates. I have learned that there are several antecedents for success that transformational collaborative teams experience. The antecedents are well-known and referenced in almost all team leadership models and training programs. Why then are teams still so prone to achieve mediocrity?

---

1 PD as an acronym is used regularly throughout this book, particularly in Chapter 6, where the purpose and processes for training middle leaders is explored in depth. It is used as a title for coordinators and teams, as well as periods of time devoted to professional development. Anything related to training is commonly referred to as PD.

HIDDEN IN PLAIN SIGHT

The starting point for any team is that each team member is unique in how they experience, process, and communicate information. Every team member differs in the role they prefer to play, as well as how they handle conflict. Middle leaders don't have the luxury of picking their team members to try to mitigate these differences. And unfortunately, teachers are not evaluated, and seldom hired, based on their ability to collaborate; however, they are strongly encouraged to collaborate, as it's in their and their students' best interests.

That latter point is why collaboration fails, regardless of how many books you read or workshops you attend. Organic collaboration is not impossible, but it needs to be the primary focus of all team members. If collaboration isn't the sole focus of everyone, then someone needs to take responsibility to align the beliefs and goals of the team. Someone needs to help team members understand their role, administrate team processes, and ensure equity among team members. Without having that someone to keep the team engaged in the collaborative work, team members will forsake team goals to pursue their own goals, specific to their unique practice and students.

Teacher-leaders, coordinators, heads of department, and vice-principals are the heart of the school; they are the someone. They are the true change agents and will be the most effective tool in ensuring transformative and sustained change. We cannot achieve all these outcomes without ensuring their buy-in and commitment to implementation. If middle leaders can understand the values that drive the beliefs and behaviors of each person, they are responsible for and to, they will prove to be much more effective in influencing outcomes.

I have written this book to help middle leaders in achieving transformational collaborative outcomes with their teams. Explained in the fourth chapter, transformational outcomes are changes in attitudes, opinions, behaviors, and practice. Research related to the impact collaboration has on affecting changes in practice and improving student learning is well-documented. Some very successfully branded books and programs based on this research go into detail about the importance of team members sharing values, beliefs, and goals, as well as about how to develop effective team processes and communication skills. Unfortunately, these books and programs rely heavily on the premise that collaboration is the responsibility of all team members, and overlook the role of the team leader in facilitating the initial stages of team development.

The educational leadership and professional learning community books and workshops don't talk about the time and effort it takes to kick-start and support collaboration. In fact, every hour of a team meeting takes two to three hours of planning and coordination to be effective. We don't work in a vacuum, and when someone has to perform cover or is just having a bad day and can't deliver on the expectations the team has set, someone has to fill that gap. Someone has to start the school year facilitating a group norming session and someone has to enforce the norms as the school year progresses, especially when team members become distracted by other priorities.

The first four chapters of this book have been purposefully laid out to provide guidance to senior leaders on how to identify, recruit, and empower middle leaders. Middle leaders can also use these chapters to assess the operating environment they are expected to succeed in. These chapters should help stoke productive conversations that clarify expectations and surface potential obstacles that senior leaders can help middle leaders mitigate.

The remaining chapters are intended to help middle leaders understand the scope of their role, clearly define the responsibilities within that scope, and provide guidance to effectively execute those responsibilities.

For example, Chapter 8 prepares middle leaders for the start of the school year. Detailed activities for each stage of team development are also provided with detailed instructions for facilitation. Each chapter will include vibrant stories of conflict and success. Besides, the activities included can be used to help teams continue their evolution and not get mired by in-team conflict or uncertainty.

This book also aims to address the frustration that every middle leader feels when they aren't quite able to practice everything they have read or learned. The success of these tools and strategies is dependent on the middle leader's ability to communicate the purpose and facilitate the process. Success shouldn't be contingent on whether senior leaders use the same strategies, nor should the use of these tools and strategies be seen as time-dependent. Over the years, it has been disheartening to hear educators say, "I can't wait to use these next year," "I wish my boss were learning this," or "This will be useful on the next team I work with." Don't hold others, or time, responsible for your ability to lead. These tools and strategies have proven successful across cultural, organizational, and curricular environments.

The beliefs, anecdotes, and tools shared in this book are the culmination of twenty years of leadership and collaborative experiences, both in the education and service industries. My journey in education began as a research assistant at the Arizona State University Child Development Laboratory, where I studied mixed-age playgroups and conducted studies of how children retain and recall information. Before moving to Asia in 1999, I worked with the Children's Action Alliance, the ARC, and the Arizona state government advocating for how to best serve children with disabilities. During these years, I developed an appreciation for working collaboratively and honed essential skills to build consensus and navigate complicated organizational hierarchies. The skills developed and experience gained during this period have helped me identify obstacles within schools that prevent transformative collaboration.

In 1999, I moved to China to teach and became quickly disenfranchised by the lack of inclusion in schools, the pressure to regurgitate scripted lesson plans, and the lack of professional development. I briefly left education in search of professional development opportunities. My ambition was quickly rewarded with team leader roles running projects that spanned Asia and fast tracked me to Senior Leadership positions. During these years, I learned how to satisfy the needs of a culturally and hierarchically diverse group of stakeholders, develop cross-cultural leadership and communication skills, and hone my experience in building effective teams.

I returned to education in 2008 and began to work with not-for-profit organizations, as well as international and Chinese bilingual schools to develop curriculum, train staff, devise parent engagement strategies, and consult senior leaders on strategy and governance. During this period, a long and mutually beneficial relationship begun with the Association of China and Mongolia International Schools (ACAMIS) and its network. Between 2011 and 2017, I worked with over two hundred private and public schools, which included surveying and facilitating workshops with over two thousand educators and administrative staff.

Four people also deserve special mention, as their support and input encouraged me to find a niche, which has become some of the most rewarding work I have done: Fritz Libby, a co-founder of Dulwich College International Management; Dr. Jim Koerschen, formerly the President of Concordia University, Ann Arbor; Tom Ulmet, Executive Director for the Association of China and Mongolia International Schools and former Superintendent of Yew Chung International Schools; and my wife, Barbara Mui, an exceptional teacher and middle

leader in her own right, who not only proofread everything I wrote, but allowed me to vicariously live through her own middle leadership successes and challenges.

SECTION 1

BUILDING THE FOUNDATION

CHAPTER 1

WHO SHOULD LEAD?

Middle leaders are the true change agents in our schools. With their buy-in and front-line perspective, they are the engines that drive transformational collaboration. Identifying the right middle leaders is not just a matter of who is ready to lead or whether they have earned it, but it is also a multi-dimensional process that requires an interdisciplinary approach. This process, when replicated across the school, will also develop an empowering culture that will enable middle leaders to thrive.

In an ideal situation, most school leaders envision teacher-led teams working in a collaborative state. The desire for this collaboration stems not only from the proven positive correlation between team collaboration and student learning but also because senior leaders need middle leaders to help them see through school improvement initiatives.

For teams to work collaboratively, interdependence among team members—by which I mean engaging in work that requires shared beliefs, goals, and, most important, trust—is essential. Working interdependently harnesses the collective knowledge of the team and broadens the perspective that can immediately be applied across classrooms, grades, and subjects. Working interdependently is also often the source of the greatest conflict. Teams that are unable to mitigate conflict, especially conflict that results from school-wide change initiatives, will become passive and retreat into silos and require senior leader intervention. When senior leaders are made aware of this type of conflict that surfaces above the team, it prevents them from orchestrating initiatives across the greater community.

A senior leader once told me, "I struggle to separate from the idea that solid recruitment negates the need for training. If we are all professional and motivated, then teams automatically should be collaborative." This statement presumes that professionalism means working collaboratively is the responsibility of an individual, or essentially, is what makes them "professional." It is also a common bias found in all organizations; if we hire professionals, they will behave professionally. This bias, though, is magnified at the middle-leader level in schools, in that senior leaders assume a team of professionals will be able to communicate effectively, keep each other motivated, and resolve their own conflicts.

> "A TEAM OF STAR PLAYERS DOES NOT MAKE AN ALL-STAR TEAM."

Two of the main antecedents for conflict are that teachers are subject-matter experts and are incredibly efficacious. These two characteristics can undermine collaboration because a teacher's individual need to succeed in their area of expertise (subject, grade level, or unique student roster) can limit their perspective and interests. They are more likely to see collaboration as a time-consuming obstacle, thus making it difficult to align with other team members and the school's strategic objectives.

> "WHEN TEACHERS COLLABORATE, THEY RUN HEADLONG INTO ENORMOUS CONFLICTS OVER PROFESSIONAL BELIEFS AND PRACTICES. IN THEIR OPTIMISM ABOUT CARING AND SUPPORTIVE COMMUNITIES, ADVOCATES OFTEN UNDERPLAY THE ROLE OF DIVERSITY, DISSENT, AND DISAGREEMENT IN COMMUNITY LIFE, LEAVING PRACTITIONERS ILL PREPARED AND CONCEPTIONS OF COLLABORATION UNDER-EXPLORED."
>
> – ACHINSTEIN, 2002

This is true of both primary and secondary teachers, especially when it comes to the topic of observations and analyzing data. A common retort I hear from teachers as to why they can't collaboratively analyze data is that since the teachers are working with different groups of students, assessment data can't inform the work of the team, only the individual teacher. I don't believe this is a coherent argument; it is rooted in something entirely unrelated—the fear of being evaluated. Truly interdependent teams, those that can't achieve their goals without the full participation of every team member, are able to distinguish feedback that broadens perspective from evaluative feedback. This distinction is very subtle, though, and without trust and a shared goal, many team members will perceive peer feedback as being critical of their practice and hence evaluative.

To overcome barriers to collaboration, senior leaders first need to acknowledge and rectify that professionalism is not the issue; the issue is aligning the interests and needs of a disparate group of individuals. Next, they need to ask: Who will take responsibility to foster interdependence among team members? Who will align the work of the team with the school's strategic objectives? Who will clarify the work of the team and the role each member plays? Who will motivate and keep the team on track? Who will mitigate conflict at the team level so that senior leadership can stay focused on the bigger picture?

Even if senior leaders have answers to these questions, or if you have been singled out as the answer to these questions, we need to next ask, "Am I the right person at this time to lead this team?" Successful leadership at any level is a multi-dimensional gambit, and ensuring the right leader is chosen requires a critical assessment on three different levels:

1.	TEAM	:	Is the team capable of working inter-dependently towards a common goal?
2.	OUTCOME	:	What is the team expected to achieve?
3.	CAPABILITY	:	What leadership characteristics are necessary at this time?

These three dimensions are not just a matter of aligning people, purpose, and time, but a way of defining the antecedents for success.

MICHAEL R. IANNINI

THREE DIMENSIONS FOR SELECTING MIDDLE LEADERS

DIMENSION 1: TEAM

Creating an ideal situation isn't just the result of all the stars aligning and shining on the middle leader. For a middle leader and the members of their team to work interdependently, it takes an incredible amount of time and team building. Unfortunately, this needed time is often not anticipated or allotted by senior leaders or the middle leaders selected to lead. In fact, I have found that, in many cases, the middle leader is chosen because they excel at their job and the senior leaders want them to "step up." The assumption is that the person being asked to step up can handle the additional responsibility. In some cases, there may be a vacancy and the prospective middle leader feels it is simply their turn; someone has to do it. In almost all appointments of middle leaders, senior leaders focus on the individual, not the context in which they are being asked to lead in. They neglect to consider the needs of the team.

Early in my leadership journey, I always thought I had all the answers. Even if I didn't, I had no problem being confident about the ones I gave. That attitude and confidence earned me a seat at the middle leaders' table, but it ultimately held me back from advancing my career. I would ensure my teams achieved what we were tasked with, but the results were often suboptimal. An example of this was when I was tasked with articulating a preschool English-language program across three different year levels. This program was managed well but poorly led. Management is one-dimensional; in this case, ensuring the teachers understood curriculum and used my lesson-planning template. Each class's result varied, though. My focus was more on achieving the senior leaders' expectations and less on including the team in the process. As I grew as a leader, I learned that if:

1. My team was familiar with and trusted each other;
2. Everyone was invested in the results of all students; and
3. The expectations for the team and each member of the team were clear, then the results would not only be more optimal but the work more rewarding.

DIMENSION 2: OUTCOME

Leadership is multi-dimensional, and in the case of the pre-school English-language program, it was a matter of achieving an outcome, ensuring all classes achieved satisfactory results. Management is getting something done, an output, and leadership is about turning those outputs into outcomes. I discuss outputs and outcomes in greater depth in Chapter 4. For the purpose of this chapter, when deciding whom we need to lead, the question that needs to be asked is whether we want someone who can get people to complete tasks, such as delivering lesson plans, or someone who can influence outcomes, which can include common planning and assessment.

The multi-dimensional nature of this project was not just a matter of teacher capability but was also impacted by grouping strategies. Furthermore, an even more important variable that needed to be considered to understand how to define success was why this project was important at that time. If I were to lead my team, I had to ensure that the senior leaders and the team agreed on how success was defined. In this case, the senior leaders wanted a leader who could engage with parents to instill confidence in the program. Grouping strategies were often influenced by parent requests, largely due to some teachers being perceived more favorably. As a middle leader, I wasn't only being asked to ensure all English program teachers were accountable for results across all year levels, but also to reduce the influence parents had on class assignments, so that grouping strategies were more in the student's best interests, not the parents.

DIMENSION 3: CAPABILITY

Have you ever worked in a school where a principal saw the school through what many assumed would be a tough leadership transition? Perhaps you were at a school where you were part of a transformative school improvement initiative. Hopefully, you have experienced being at a school where senior leaders supported and empowered you. These three situations require three very different types of leadership: transitional leadership, transformative leadership, and supportive leadership. This does not constitute the definitive list of leadership types, but these situations do require leaders to embody distinctly different characteristics and employ different strategies.

It would not be reasonable to think any one person would be equally successful in each of those three situations. While we do ask this of our senior leaders, it is not reasonable to expect it from our middle leaders. Thus, we should differentiate our approach in choosing middle leaders and recruit candidates that have experience and skill sets that are commensurate with the team they will lead, the outcome they will be expected to achieve, and the stage of development the school or team are in. To do this, we need to find leaders that are the right fit for these three dimensions and clearly define the role of the middle leader in line with those dimensional considerations. We also need to ensure their buy-in to the outcome that is being sought.

When reflecting on this case and why I was asked to lead the articulation project, I realize it wasn't because of my background in child development, but because of my interpersonal skills. This project required someone to:

1. Build a team across grade levels,
2. Engage with parents and focus them on supporting their child, and
3. Focus on the people, not curriculum.

This experience allowed me to grow as a leader and achieve larger long-term outcomes. I empowered learning assistants to lead non-English lessons, enabling the lead teachers to float across classes and observe other English lessons. I worked with curriculum coordinator to identify activities teachers could introduce to parents to support language learning, which improved parents' perception of teachers. Lastly, when any student struggled, teachers across year levels would meet to understand the student's current trajectory and what their role would be to improve it.

These three dimensions (team, outcome, and capability) now become the basis for selecting the middle leader. Multi-dimensional assessments require multiple perspectives; therefore, an interdisciplinary recruitment process is required to identify the right leadership candidates.

3 DIMENSIONAL SELECTION CRITERIA

TEAM
- How familiar are the team members with one another?
- Have they successfully demonstrated working interdependently?
- Are they invested in the results of each other's students?

OUTCOME
- Is the reason for the desired outcome clear?
- What will it look like when the desired outcome is achieved?
- Is there coherency with the tasks identified to achieve the outcome?

CAPABILITY
- What competencies does the middle leader need to develop the team?
- What competencies does the middle leader need to complete the tasks?
- What competencies does the middle leader need to realize the outcome?

CLARIFYING THE ROLE

Unfortunately, the selection process for middle leaders is often limited to only senior leaders and not allotted sufficient time to seek feedback from other relevant stakeholders. This happens because one school year hasn't finished, but preparations for the next school year have begun. In the myriad pressing tasks, most senior leaders will not take time to critically assess who should be the middle leader, let alone account for the time it takes to prepare middle leaders for their role in the coming year. Even if there is no change in grade level leader or department head roles, we should not assume the next school year will be business as usual.

In my interactions with middle leaders, I am struck by how many don't have job descriptions or amended working agreements to account for their additional duties. Furthermore, where job descriptions exist, they are often vague. Some senior leaders may even become defensive if questioned about their expectations regarding the role. Left with this lack of clarity, middle leaders new to a team or school often have to learn about the job through the age-old orientation method known as, *"That's just how we do things around here."* The number of schools that treat teacher-led role descriptions like a legend that gets handed down from generation to generation is unnerving. It is for this reason, whether or not the middle leader has a full-time teaching role, that they should still have their job description evaluated and amended to clearly define the leadership responsibilities they are assuming, as well as create buy-in to their expected outcomes. Also, even if they are returning to a leadership position, we must consider the three dimensions and adjust the job description accordingly.

Outcomes, which will be further explored in Chapter 4, are long-term strategic objectives we plan to achieve, typically in three to five years. During this period, it is reasonable to assume that teams will require different styles of leadership to achieve the desired outcome. The leader who begins the journey may not be the right leader to end it, but that doesn't mean they can't still be part of the journey. Initially, teams will require someone who has great organizational skills and is attuned to the needs of each team member. As the team grows and becomes more interdependent, it will then require a leader who promotes risk-taking and can stay focused on the big picture. As the team closes in on their desired outcome, they will finally need someone to monitor and evaluate progress and keep the team motivated. Even with the outcome fully achieved, we will require a different style of leadership, someone who can consolidate the achievements and scale the impact.

Let's now consider how to use an interdisciplinary approach to recruit middle leaders, regardless of if they are new to a team or returning to a leadership role. Here are three essential questions that require input from multiple stakeholders:

1. Does this candidate have the resources and relationships necessary to achieve the desired outcome?
2. Does this candidate have the experience and interpersonal skills to foster a culture of interdependency within the team?
3. Does this candidate have the same skills and attributes as other middle leaders who have successfully achieved similar outcomes?

These will also help identify what support middle leaders need so they can begin preparing for next year.

When you take time to ask the right questions with an interdisciplinary team and assess how the next school year may differ from this one (team composition, accreditation, new goals, etc.), you will next need to review the position description and either edit it in line with next year's reality or reaffirm the expectations for the middle leaders based on this year's achievements. The position description should be viewed as a living document, which becomes an opportunity to raise the bar, as well as confirm the middle leader's acceptance of the expectations being put on them. This is the most important part of achieving buy-in, and once buy-in is achieved, you will find your middle leaders more accommodating and resilient to the unforeseen challenges that will inevitably occur in the new school year.

CHAPTER 2

WHERE MIDDLE LEADERS THRIVE: SEEDING THE CULTURE

What does it mean to be Professional?

The last chapter ended with three key questions senior leaders across the school need to consider when selecting middle leaders for specific teams and departments. The reason for involving multiple leaders is twofold: first, the middle leader needs to work productively with administrators in different roles, and second, they need to ensure the work of their team aligns with and supports whole school objectives. However, selecting the right leader is not just a matter of having the right experience and interpersonal skills; they also need to share commonly understood values and beliefs with their team and the stakeholders they will be engaging with.

> "IF WE HIRE PROFESSIONALS, THEY SHOULD ACT PROFESSIONALLY."
>
> – PRIMARY DEPUTY PRINCIPAL, BEIJING, CHINA

Professionalism is a subjective value that can greatly influence the culture of a team and school. A simple method to understand how labeling a behavior as professional or not professional influences culture would be to ask each team member to identify attributes associated with highly professional people. The result of this activity will yield some overlap of identified attributes, but more importantly, it will reveal disparity. This notion of professionalism, particularly the disparity in how each team member defines professionalism, becomes a significant issue when conflict arises. The disparity in how professionalism is defined can largely be attributed to the values and beliefs we hold for how a professional should act. Words, such as professionalism, cannot be taken at face value and are symptomatic of a much greater intercultural dilemma that senior leaders are not prepared to cope with alone.

Collaboration, for example, is a value that can be demonstrated in different ways, from cooperatively sharing lesson plans to observing colleagues and giving them feedback to broaden their perspective on the effectiveness of their instruction. If we want to recruit "professional" and "collaborative" staff, we need to ensure we have a common understanding of what those values mean and the behaviors that demonstrate those values, and then ensure existing and future staff measure up to those values through the demonstration of relevant and desired behaviors.

The attributes associated with being professional or collaborating will vary from culture to culture. In Chapter 8, I introduce an activity, based on Implicit Leadership Belief Theory, that not only helps teams build consensus on a definition for effective team leadership, but also provides greater background on this theory. I have worked with several schools that have wanted to foster greater collaboration, but have ignored this underlying cultural divide, the disparity in the expectations colleagues hold for each other that exists in all schools. Senior leaders try to fill the divide by mandating teams to identify curricular goals, based on the assumption that curriculum is a common touch point for all team members and something that they should all believe is essential. However, curriculum is a set of guidelines, and our values and beliefs will largely determine how we interpret and implement it.

Don't Let Curriculum Define Your Team Culture

In my observations, curriculum tends to be the source of greatest conflict because of the disparity between professional beliefs and practices. An example of this type of conflict, with International Baccalaureate schools, is the requirement to develop the dispositions and skills in students that will support more effective agents of learning. At the same time, teaching staff are being pushed to develop more structured and consistent language practices. For many educators, these two requirements conflict in that some educators prefer greater structure, whereas others want to have greater license to achieve the required learning objectives.

Yes, curriculum is something we all have in common, but you need shared values and beliefs to pursue transformative goals. Putting curriculum at the center of the work that teams engage in will undermine the culture of a team and lead to overly broad or very transactional goals. The reason for this is twofold, firstly within any team there is varying degrees of experience with curriculum and varying needs of students across classes, and therefore teachers may have different priorities for what aspect of curriculum they want and need to attend to. Secondly, if team members don't understand or appreciate "why" their priorities conflict they may make unfair value assessments about each other, which in turn undermines trust and the ability to collaborate meaningfully.

Therefore, when taking culture into consideration, and trying to foster a culture of transformative collaboration, a balance needs to be struck between identifying an area of development where individual team members can pursue individual inquiries and ensure that whatever is discovered at the individual level can contribute to the development of all team members. The solution in this case is not curricular, though this is where most senior leaders gravitate, because it is the most tangible. Focusing only on what we can see and touch effectively reinforces transactional and superficial cultures.

It is also common for senior leaders to try to corral all teams into large initiatives and hold them accountable to the same processes and timelines. Though it can be easily rationalized that we all need to be moving in the same direction, these initiatives are largely conceived from a single perspective and administered with very few resources (technology, time, training, support staff, etc.). If all teams were equal in their stage of development and had shared values and beliefs, then we could hold staff accountable to the same goals and achieve large initiatives.

Unfortunately, not all teams are equal, nor will all teams respond similarly to a commonly understood objective. Teams move in and out of different stages, so we can't hold all teams accountable to the same expectations and administrative processes. To begin building the foundation for collaborative, transformative, and sustainable change in schools, senior leaders need to not only make the values that drive their vision explicit, but they also need to review pedagogical and administrative practices that affect the work of teams. To sustain a culture that will drive strategic initiatives, we need to accept that not everyone is positioned to equally contribute to the overall outcome. We need to differentiate the expectations for each team and place people on those teams who are suited for those expectations. This does not mean we have remedial and advanced teams. Differentiation, in this case acknowledges that each staff member:

1. Views the school differently, relative to their work and relationship with stakeholders,
2. Has different interests and ambitions, and
3. Depending on the time of year, as well as curricular responsibilities, their capacity to take on new work will vary.

So, how do we assemble these teams and recruit new staff to our school to bring fresh perspectives?

A transformational collaborative culture is built through fostering a network of interdependent relationships. These relationships, though, require a high degree of trust and shared values and beliefs. As I will demonstrate in this chapter, not everyone may be suited for your vision, and to achieve that vision may require making changes to the team from year to year. I realize that most team leaders, as well as senior leaders, don't have the luxury of switching people in and out of teams; however, the process I am going to introduce is not only for identifying who is right for the team but also how we can define a culture that will foster transformational collaboration. Even though we may not have much flexibility with grade-level and subject teams, there is ample evidence of interdisciplinary teams playing a larger role in school improvement initiatives. One example of an interdisciplinary team that I discuss in greater detail in Chapter 3 is the Middle Leadership Team. However, for these teams to thrive, there needs to be a culture that reinforces shared values and ensures buy-in to an initiative's core purpose.

To build this culture, let's first consider how schools are organized. Let's start with the premise that teachers attend regular meetings for different teams over the course of a school year, but there may only be one team they contribute significantly to. Also, some teams may be very early in their development, so we need to be realistic about what we can expect of that team, let alone what goals the team leader should be expected to personally achieve. When we assess teams from a multi-dimensional perspective, we gain a greater appreciation for the role they can play in contributing to the school's core purpose. Senior leaders need to accept that not all teams are ready to pursue the strategic objectives set. But this does not mean all staff are incapable of contributing toward achieving those objectives.

Let's now build on a common organizational strategy where grade-level and subject teams are for planning. Let's fix the role and expectations of those teams to that purpose alone and then consider other or new teams for transformational initiatives. If you can accept this suggestion, then also consider that not every teacher should have to be on a transformation team, as some teachers will rightly be overwhelmed in their current role.

In Jim Collins' *Good to Great* framework, this is Stage 1:

> "THOSE WHO BUILD GREAT ORGANIZATIONS MAKE SURE THEY HAVE THE RIGHT PEOPLE ON THE BUS, THE WRONG PEOPLE OFF THE BUS, AND THE RIGHT PEOPLE IN THE KEY SEATS BEFORE THEY FIGURE OUT WHERE TO DRIVE THE BUS."

Once we have a general organizational outline of what teams we have, as well as a general idea of what teams we need to form, let's apply the lessons from Chapter 1 to identify who will lead the transformational change teams. To identify the right leaders, for the transformational change teams, we need to consider how this team will be composed, clearly articulate its purpose and identify the resources and support the team will need. Additionally, the prospective middle leader has to reflect on the role they are taking and agree to the outcome the team is expected to achieve. Both senior leaders and middle leaders, in order to achieve the agreed-upon outcome, need to ensure *cultural fit:*

> "CULTURAL FIT IS THE LIKELIHOOD THAT SOMEONE WILL REFLECT AND/OR BE ABLE TO ADAPT TO THE CORE BELIEFS, ATTITUDES, AND BEHAVIORS THAT MAKE UP YOUR ORGANIZATION.... EMPLOYEES WHO FIT WELL WITH THEIR ORGANIZATION, CO-WORKERS, AND SUPERVISOR HAD GREATER JOB SATISFACTION, WERE MORE LIKELY TO REMAIN WITH THEIR ORGANIZATION, AND SHOWED SUPERIOR JOB PERFORMANCE."
>
> – KATIE BOUTON, HARVARD BUSINESS REVIEW

In defining cultural fit, and especially the process for establishing teams, we should put less emphasis on curricular outcomes and pay more attention to skills and behaviors that will improve a team's ability to work interdependently. A culturally fit team would then be one composed of members who have common values and beliefs and the capacity to pursue a common interest. The process for ensuring fit requires us to develop a team leader profile specific to the outcomes that team is expected to achieve. The team leader profile is crucial to ensuring that not only is the team leader *fit* for the prospective team, but, more important, the team leader naturally reinforces the values and demonstrates the behaviors of the underlying culture.

When considering a process for team leader recruitment and evaluation, you must include feedback from the team, as each team is unique in its membership and challenges. If a team is expecting to lose a team leader who has been a good facilitator and helped team members resolve conflict, then it is in that team's best interest to contribute feedback on prospective candidates. A practical way to build the profile for a fit candidate would be to:

1. Assemble a group that is representative of the team and other leaders that will work with this team;
2. Ask each person to first consider and define their relationship to this candidate in terms of Purpose, Values and Behavior:

    - PURPOSE : defines how and what this person is expected to achieve with the prospective team leader,

- VALUES : identifies core beliefs that supports the purpose, and
- BEHAVIORS : these are the work and communication styles that they hope the prospective team leader will demonstrate, which should also be aligned with the identified values.

3. Build consensus on a position description that synthesizes each team member's responses for the purpose, values, and behaviors as they relate to the prospective team leader.

Multi-stakeholder Selection Process

The result of this interdisciplinary approach will provide a profile that defines the candidate's unique role that directly supports the team culture and indirectly contributes to the school culture. This exercise will also give insight into how the team culture is changing and, when extrapolated across teams, how the school culture is changing as a result of new challenges or opportunities.

Ensuring a candidate is culturally fit also requires good intuition and excellent questioning skills—to understand and focus on what breeds success in the culture being sought. Achieving that level of understanding requires a range of input from stakeholders with varying skill sets. This interdisciplinary approach also helps us to prevent silos developing within the school, as we will be ensuring that new recruits are capable of demonstrating the values and behaviors that will foster strong relationships across the school.

Here are a few questions that will help assess cultural fit in an interview:

- What type of culture do you thrive in?
- What values do you feel support our guiding statements?
- What behaviors demonstrate those values?
- What values are you drawn to and how would they be reflected in your ideal workplace?
- How would you describe our culture based on what you know?
- How does this align with the work culture you are seeking?

- What best practices would you bring with you from a previous job? Do you see yourself being able to implement these best practices in our school culture?
- Tell me about a time when you worked for a school where you felt you were not a strong cultural fit. Why was it a bad fit and how did you adapt?

"I would never let HR participate in recruiting or evaluating my teachers" is a common sentiment I hear in schools. I won't argue that educators are incapable of being effective recruiters—in fact, many pride themselves on it—but the recruitment and evaluation systems for a school looking to achieve transformative outcomes shouldn't solely be grounded in pedagogical practices, and definitely shouldn't be facilitated by a single person. Collaboration is something that has driven innovation across industries, and it is not pedagogical. To achieve the level of differentiation I am advocating for—to achieve cultural fit—senior leaders need to empower middle management to play a larger role in organizational management, including recruitment and evaluation. Collaboration can be a transformational outcome achieved and demonstrated by the combined outputs of leaders, at all levels across the school. It is not only the result of senior leaders coordinating with school-wide stakeholders for recruiting the right people for the right teams, but also team leaders coordinating activities that build trust and connect the activities of their team to the objectives of the school.

As you begin to define the optimal culture for the team, and specifically the team leader profile, the criteria for assessing who fits become much narrower. As the criteria narrow, there is a tendency for the interviewer to ask questions that are too specific, limiting the breadth of responses and informing the candidate of the required response. A well-intentioned example of trying to assess facilitation skills is: "What are important traits for a good facilitator, and can you provide an example of when you demonstrated those traits?" This question will yield very little insight into a candidate's ability to be a successful facilitator for the team that they will join.

Instead, using the questions above, develop a series of questions where facilitation is the subject of inquiry, such as:

1. Think of someone you know who is an excellent facilitator. What underlying values, do you believe, supported that person's work as a facilitator?
2. What behaviors demonstrate those values?
3. How does this align with the work culture you are seeking?

Additionally, many of these questions are value-based, so we need to control for the possibility that the interviewer does not share the same values as the team being recruited for. The interdisciplinary approach will help us control for that by ensuring that the team leader profile synthesizes multiple perspectives, and, when appropriate, the candidate is being interviewed by people with differing perspectives.

Use a Team to Select Team Leaders

Leaders at all levels can learn to be better interviewers, but an interdisciplinary approach is a far more effective strategy, especially when those involved have a stake in the team's success. Schools that have professional learning communities (PLC[2]) or study teams should form an interdisciplinary team with shared decision-making that will recruit team leaders and members for teams that are being asked to achieve transformative outcomes. Furthermore, by using a team approach to recruit, and fostering interdependency in the process, you will also be demonstrating collaboration, something that will be visible to all members participating in this process. Participants in this process should understand and experience that they are not being selected to work in a grade level or department, but they are being selected to achieve a transformational outcome aligned with the school's guiding statements.

---

[2] I use this acronym throughout the book. There are many types of professional learning communities and I do not subscribe to any one of them. I use this term in a general sense to refer to a group of teachers that have been assigned to a team to explore some area of practice.

CHAPTER 3

THE SILO DILEMMA

A puzzle can only be solved when the pieces are put together. Schools are like unsolved puzzles and the pieces are its teams, which individually only provide a small piece of the picture. When the teams are connected, the larger picture starts to come into focus.

Middle management is a multi-dimensional role, and success in this role is directly related to the organizational culture. In the first chapter, we explored how the three dimensions of *Team, Outcome,* and *Capability* affect middle management, and in the second chapter, I highlighted the importance of using an interdisciplinary approach to recruit and evaluate middle leaders, specifically to ensure perspectives for all three dimensions.

For senior leaders reading this, your job is only half done. In this chapter, I explain how to scale network effects for middle leaders. For middle leaders reading this, we are going to be adding a fourth dimension critical for success. This fourth dimension is assuming accountability for the whole school. To achieve the network effect and assume accountability, we need to solve the puzzle known as the Silo Dilemma.

The Silo Dilemma is the result of teams building up walls between themselves and other grades and departments, based on the belief that unless their peers share a subject, student, or similar work task, they can't collaborate. You can't foster collaboration within a team, let alone across teams, if there are no shared beliefs or values. These silos make it even more difficult to support individual teams struggling to collaborate.

A breakdown at the team level will most likely occur because of problems occurring in the silo, and the silo walls will act as an obstacle preventing meaningful intervention. Teams that operate in a culture that reinforces silos are limited to cooperative tasks, such as organizing and channeling resources and information. Teams that only serve as a unit of organization are in fact working groups, as defined by reWork's Project Aristotle. This was a study funded by Google with the intended purpose of identifying what makes for an effective team.

I have observed in many "silo" schools a teacher-led team's ability to plan units of instruction, facilitate assessments, and collaborate to resolve immediate concerns about students. The teacher-leader and team members are paid to do a job, they love their work, and they get *their* jobs done so they can feel a sense of accomplishment, or what several researchers refer to as the need to realize self-efficacy. This team, in a silo environment, is the exception, not the norm, because they have persevered to transcend the attitude of "this is how things get done around here."

Unfortunately, though, this team's achievements will be limited in scope, scale, and duration. This same team, if placed in a school that nurtured a transformational collaborative culture (to be defined in Chapter 4), could be more confident and motivated to investigate the root causes that impede learning across the whole school and engage other teams in dialogue that produces positive long-term outcomes schoolwide.

The following story is based on work I did with a secondary leadership team. It is an example of how this team began to emerge from the Silo Dilemma:

> *A secondary head of department shared his concern about a few students he felt could not pass their upcoming A-Level math exam. When this issue surfaced, other team members immediately identified with the same concern and knew who those students were; they also shared the same concerns that those students would have difficulty in other subjects.*
>
> *Immediately, members of the team felt connected and relieved that they didn't have to confront the problem alone. The team began discussing possible intervention, but lamented that they couldn't have identified these concerns earlier. The discussion of intervention slowly evolved into creating hypotheses, such as, "If we work with primary and successive grades to identify student performance issues earlier, then we could intervene and shape this trajectory before it becomes an eleventh-hour emergency."*
>
> *The discussion identified several challenges, primarily that coordinating such a feat would be beyond their means. Not only did the requisite relationship with the primary section not exist, but a few team leaders would be leaving the school in the next year and there wasn't enough time allotted in the schedule to accommodate the number of meetings and research required to build those bridges.*
>
> *However, the meeting concluded with a sense of progress, as the team member who initiated the discussion no longer felt*

alone in having to solve this problem. Additionally, short-term collaborative activities were planned to quickly intervene and provide additional support for the students. It should also be noted that this conversation only transpired as a result of the department heads' participation in training. They wouldn't have had enough time to collaboratively resolve a mutual concern if it hadn't surfaced during a professional development period.

The case above demonstrates that teams can emerge from their silos, as well as how interdisciplinary teams can promote transformative collaboration. This *ad hoc* team of department heads emerging from the silo also demonstrates the importance of defining a purpose and setting sights on achieving an outcome. Now that the team has emerged from the silo, the process of identifying who will take them to the next stage of development needs to be answered. Who will mobilize them as a team and coordinate their work? Who will take responsibility for developing an empowering environment for them to succeed as a team? Does a team of leaders need a team leader?

The Middle Leadership Team

Leadership roles attract some of the most curious, ambitious, and growth-minded individuals. These are three vital attributes for achieving transformational change. When people with these attributes are put together, there will be a multiplier effect of new ideas that improve practice. Why then, after the team leader and coordinator roles are assigned, are schools not realizing this multiplier effect? What practical strategies are senior leadership teams lacking to empower middle leaders and foster collaboration as a larger network? Why do great leadership candidates retreat to silos and await their marching orders?

Let's first assess the question of why our middle leaders don't feel empowered enough to emerge from the silos. These ascending leaders have, either through curiosity, career-mindedness, or even coercion, accepted a role that is poorly defined, has limited or no authority, and comes with a huge target for colleagues to set their sights on. The expressions "Don't shoot the messenger" and "We are all in this together" are common mottos for these people. These are the middle leaders: the grade-level and subject team leaders, department heads, coordinators, and any other role tasked with making sure a group of staff use time and resources appropriately and productively.

I give credit to senior leaders for recognizing the importance of middle leaders in affecting change across a school, but middle leaders need to be appropriately equipped to ensure desired changes stick; they need to be capacity-built to sustain change.[3] To build capacity to affect meaningful change, middle leaders need three to five years with their team, with the first year being spent mostly forming the team, developing a collaborative network, and capacity-building the team to achieve the desired change. This is different from the current reality, where most schools have a revolving door of middle leaders, often caused by competing school initiatives and high turnover. This periodical assignment of team leaders is like playing musical chairs: each time the music stops, teams are forced to redevelop.

When I confront senior leaders regarding the lack of continuity in leadership, they often justify hasty leadership assignments because the nature of change is urgent and/or the person chosen has significant experience. Schools are time-poor as it is; throw in urgency and it's a cocktail for disenfranchisement. In addition, relying on experience as a solution has limited success, as no manner of change is ever the same. Experience may help some leaders understand how to navigate the school hierarchy, but if a lot of the "experience" these leaders have gained is "getting things done," then it's a good bet their teams aren't collaborating and the product of what they produce will be one-dimensional, driven from the perspective of the team leader.

Middle leaders are often selected for their technical or organizational capabilities, not their interpersonal or networking skills. Like many staff in schools, middle leaders feel isolated, with no clear understanding of how they can collaborate with each other. Outside of their team, their relationships with leadership are linear and often limited to reporting. As such, the type of collaboration occurring in their team is often linear and limited to reporting. This linear

---

3 Capacity-building is a term I use regularly in this book. That will be explored in detail in Chapter 6, as to how we can develop or build the capacity of middle leaders, to assume a larger role with greater responsibility to their team.

relationship model is principally responsible for creating and reinforcing the silos.

If middle leaders are asked why they don't collaborate with each other, they often make the same excuses that members of their team make about collaboration: "we have different students," "we plan differently," and "we do not have time." These are, unfortunately, valid excuses in time-starved environments. Even if time could be "made," if people aren't trained and disciplined in using that time appropriately, odds are the time "made" will be used to catch up on work, not collaborate.

If successfully managing change or developing a collaborative culture is vital to the school's success, then creating a **Middle Leadership Team** is essential. We need middle leaders buy-in and front-line perspective to affect transformative change. If you accept that this role is critical to developing a collaborative network in the school, then you need to formally establish a middle leadership team. As a separate team, middle leaders will provide critical peer support and be able to experience the practice of crossbreeding ideas insulated from the naysayers scattered across the school.

Matrix Organizational Structure

> "TOP MANAGEMENT TEAMS CAN NOT AFFORD TO LET ALL DAY-TO-DAY OPERATIONAL COORDINATION ISSUES ESCALATE UPWARD. ITS REAL CHALLENGE IS TO ACHIEVE LATERAL COORDINATION ALSO AT THE LEVELS BELOW. THIS CAN BE ACHIEVED THROUGH HARD-WIRING OR SOFT-WIRING. A MATRIX STRUCTURE IS AN EXAMPLE OF HARD-WIRING, BECAUSE THE TWO BOSSES OF A MANAGER IN A MATRIXED POSITION HAVE THE JOINT RESPONSIBILITY TO SET HIS OBJECTIVES, SUPERVISE HIS WORK, DO HIS APPRAISAL, AND ENSURE HIS DEVELOPMENT."
>
> — MAKING MATRIX ORGANIZATIONS ACTUALLY WORK, BY HERMAN VANTRAPPEN AND FREDERIC WIRTZ, MARCH 01, 2016, HARVARD BUSINESS REVIEW.

To empower the middle leadership team to collaborate, this would require either subject, grade-level, and department teams meeting less or freeing up additional periods for middle leaders. This is not impossible, if the subject, grade, and department teams are formed solely to operate as what Google identified as working groups. Then they don't require that much time; they just need to learn to use time more effectively.

For schools invested into PLCs, the middle leadership team could be a PLC unit. The reward is capacity-building a team that will act as a firewall for senior leadership, shielding them from the various types of conflict within teams that isolated middle leaders struggle to cope with. Middle leadership teams help prevent issues from escalating by collectively addressing organizational conflict.

These teams also serve as a benchmark for teams across the school to assess their own progress, thus ensuring greater continuity across the school. This continuity adds to the clarity of purpose and further aids the development of other teams. The middle leadership team now becomes a forum for sharing best practices at an organizational level as well as an important pillar that supports a collaborative culture.

If you agree with this assessment, let's now discuss a solution. The middle leadership team is not a new concept; it has been around for decades and is the lynchpin to the matrix organizational structure:

> *A matrix structure does not solve all problems, and in fact, can create new ones, but more efficient and effective lateral coordination ensures everyone has a seat at the table. The matrix structure also reinforces interdisciplinary cooperation among leadership, as multiple leaders are now accountable for how teams perform across the school. Additionally, because most, if not all, school reform initiatives are top-down-driven, with little input from the middle, the matrix structure can empower the middle to channel input to senior leadership.*
>
> *For example, to ensure the latest innovative curricular initiatives like STEM and PBL take root, they require matrix organizational constructs. These initiatives not only require interdisciplinary unit planning, but they also require that multiple teams be accountable for student performance. Schools are ripe for a hybrid matrix structure that doesn't require middle leaders to assume reporting responsibilities with staff in different*

teams, but does require leadership across the school spending more time understanding what is going on in different teams.

Every senior leader I work with praises their school's middle leadership in one breath and expresses frustration in the next. Teaching and planning are only half of the job, and the rest falls on the administration to ensure school initiatives are far-reaching. At the senior leadership level, the picture is clear, but to those below, it is difficult to connect the dots. That exhale of frustration, then, is senior leadership's angst from the myriad problems middle leadership approach them with. Matrix organizations help to alleviate this frustration, as they were born from companies seeking to break down silos and force middle leaders to coordinate the goals and activities with staff that have responsibilities to different teams. To achieve this level of coordination, you need a middle leadership team.

School-wide Initiatives Hinge on Middle Leaders' Buy-in and Common Understanding

The type of middle leadership team that does exist in schools is far from what I have begun to describe. Senior leaders often assemble their middle leaders to disseminate important information, give instructions, or ask for feedback. The problem with these meetings is they are *ad hoc* and the people in these meetings don't feel they are part of a team; therefore, they interpret information or instructions specific to their context, and not in terms of how it should be applied to the school. Team leaders walk away from these meetings with different understandings and varying degrees of buy-in. Those differences are ultimately the antecedents to failure.

Imagine a scenario where the middle leaders are assembled, and instead of being talked at, they are given tools and time to collaboratively process and build consensus on what is being disseminated. If the meetings are *ad hoc* and those in attendance have no formal affiliation with each other, then collaboratively processing information can be time-consuming, with no guarantee of achieving buy-in or consensus. This is not to say the meeting won't be productive, but it may take several iterations to achieve the desired outcome.

However, if the participants assembled are part of a team that has undergone forming activities, such as agreeing on group norms and decision-making processes, and have learned to accommodate each other's different communication and working styles, then these meetings will require less instances and less time and have a higher chance of achieving the desired outcome.

This being said, a high-functioning team can be efficient and productive, but if the desired outcome is not clearly communicated or is unrealistic, even the best teams will struggle and likely retreat to their silo. The success of the middle leadership team, like any team, hinges not only on having a common understanding of what needs to be done and buy-in from each member, but also clarity of purpose. Purpose, or mission, born of vision, is not only required to initiate action, but is also essential to understanding how to evaluate the outcome. To achieve a common understanding of what needs to be done and buy in to it, people need to know *why* they should be doing something.

Doing something is why I wrote this book. I want schools to do something *amazing*. To achieve something amazing, I contend that capacity-building middle leaders to empower teams *across* the school is the key to the transformational change that I will define in the next chapter. Schools do a lot of *somethings*, but all their somethings aren't transformational. The somethings they do are the same somethings they have always done.

Sure, adjustments are made along the way, but true transformative improvements in student learning are rare. Here is an example of this vicious something circle: in the West, we are killing ourselves to copy the somethings (killer math results) done in the East, and in the East, they want to replicate *our* somethings (creativity). The somethings I refer to are outputs. We know they are important, but what outcome is sought? The problem is a pronounced misunderstanding between outputs and outcomes, the subject of the next chapter.

CHAPTER 4
OUTPUTS VS OUTCOMES

The Collaboration Spectrum

Many teachers and administrators feel they collaborate effectively. Several engage in common planning activities. Some engage with peers to present work and solicit feedback. A few even meet to analyze data and identify areas for improvement with the intent to improve each other's practice. The activities I just described are what I consider to be part of the collaboration spectrum.

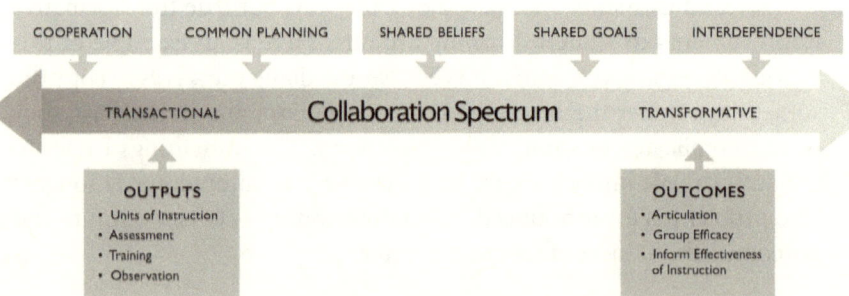

This spectrum has two ends: transactional and transformative. At the transactional end of the spectrum is the work that teams are expected to deliver, their deliverables, and be evaluated on, such as common planning activities and presenting work for feedback.

On the transformative end of the spectrum, teams engage in values-based activities that influence positive changes in attitudes, behavior, and knowledge, or what I refer to as *transformative collaboration*. Team members work interdependently and believe they have a responsibility for all students', not just theirs.

Transactional and transformational collaboration is best understood by understanding the difference between outputs and outcomes. I consider transactions, or more specifically tasks, such as lesson planning and grading, as outputs. Outputs are products of a defined process that individuals can often deliver on their own. They may need supervision and instruction to understand the process, but once they have the necessary knowledge, they should be able to produce the desired outputs. Outcomes, on the other hand, are the culmination of multiple outputs resulting in less tangible products.

Below is a table of transformational outcomes, organized by Short, Mid and Long term. Short-term transformational outcomes can take anywhere from one to two years to achieve. Mid-term outcomes can take between 2 and 5 years to be achieved. Long-term outcomes, or effectively what every school espouses in its Guiding Statements, are changes to value and belief systems that we may never be able to measure, but what many schools aspire to influence.

Transformational Outcomes = Impact		
SHORT	MID	LONG
Knowledge Attitudes Skills Opinions Motivation	Action Behavior Practice Decision Making	Social Economic Civic Environmental

Defining Collaboration

How do you define collaboration? Does the result of your collaborative work improve instructional and operational effectiveness? *If you are satisfied with how your team is performing, then the expectation for what your team can achieve may be too low.* The expectations for a team that is working collaboratively can vary greatly and will determine the amount of support team members require to work interdependently.

For example, if the goal is for teams to support an accreditation process, then the support is limited to ensuring clarity regarding roles and responsibilities, and the expected results are tangible. Interdependence is not a necessary outcome and the desired result is merely transactional, regardless of how arduous the tasks are. However, if the goal is to achieve curricular articulation, then working interdependently is a necessary outcome and the team will require more support and resources. In the first scenario, the objective is to align team members, and collaboration is the result of supervision. In the second scenario, collaboration is member-driven, but facilitated by a team leader. The first scenario is an example of transactional collaboration and the latter is an example of transformational collaboration.

To further illustrate the difference between transactional and transformational collaboration, let's examine Maxim Sytch's research on three models of interdependence and the coordination tools that evidence the model being demonstrated. Based on the ideas of Maxim Sytch, an Associate Professor at the University of Michigan, the image below is from a presentation and is available online in his *coursera.org* course, *Leading Teams.*

Required Coordination Tools

Pooled Interdependence

Sequential Interdependence

Reciprocal Interdependence

LOW
Coordination Demands

Standardize requirements for process and outputs

Planning and scheduling (centralized coordination can work)

Continuous information flows, group meetings, multiple integrators

HIGH
Coordination Demands

The first model of interdependence is *Pooled Interdependence*, which I believe most clearly demonstrates what transactional collaboration looks like. This is also the simplest style of leadership, where **the team leader delegates tasks to individual team members and follows up with them directly**. Instead of leading a team, the team leader is supervising several individuals who are not accountable to each other or the team. An example of this form of interdependence would be team members individually completing lesson plans with the overall objective being that the team has demonstrated that all grade levels or subjects are compliant with curriculum.

The second model of interdependence, *Sequential Interdependence*, is representative of a team that has a shared goal that requires a number of outputs to demonstrate achieving the shared goal. The subtle distinction between this form of interdependence and Pooled Interdependence is that in the first model the team members have a shared responsibility, but in this model, they share a goal that requires planning and coordination. An example of this would be common planning and team members taking responsibility for completing different units and sharing them with the team. This requires a high degree of trust and confidence in each team member, but does not necessarily require them to provide feedback to each other or observe how each other facilitates the lessons.

The final model of interdependence, *Reciprocal Interdependence*, is the true embodiment of transformational collaboration. If we agree that fostering interdependence is critical to achieving transformational collaboration, then we need to support and empower middle leaders to achieve Reciprocal Interdependence within their teams. To achieve this, we need to give team leaders, and teams, more time for planning and engaging in the types of activities representative of this form of interdependence, such as classroom observations and interdisciplinary planning.

Outcomes-based education is not new to educators. However, challenging educators to apply the principles and practices to their own work, and that of their teams, is something I do not see often in schools. Some educators claim their teams are high-functioning, collaborative, and outcome-focused, but in my opinion, these teams seem more efficient and effective at the output end of the spectrum. Their meeting agendas and how they plan, report, and make decisions evidence this. They plan and coordinate with zeal and show a high degree of trust in each other's individual performance, but the discussions often are limited to tasks or never evolve beyond a generative stage.

In Chapter 7, I further elaborate that **transactional collaboration doesn't require leadership, only effective management and supervision**. Pooled Interdependent teams aren't teams at all, they are work groups that only require a supervisor. Pooled Interdependent work groups will demonstrate less conflict largely because team members are less reliant on one another. The task and the deliverable are well-understood and there are fewer interactions to manage. Outcomes, however, are the result of multiple outputs and require a greater degree of coordination, investment of time, and input by multiple stakeholders and outcomes relevant to the work of their team. It is for this reason that **Reciprocally Interdependent teams need an effective team leader**.

Differentiating Outputs from Outcomes

To further illustrate the difference between Outputs and Outcomes, please review this worksheet I introduce in my Goal Setting classes. This worksheet was adapted from the "Outcomes vs. Outputs" section of *Innovation Network's Logic Model Workbook (p. 17)*. The entire workbook is available for free by registering on *www.innonet.org* and from PowerPoint presentation slides created by Taylor-Powell, E., & Henert, E. (2008), *Developing a logic model*.

HIDDEN IN PLAIN SIGHT

	EXAMPLES	WHAT EXAMPLES ARE RELEVANT TO YOUR TEAM?
OUTPUTS *The direct and measurable products of a program's activities or services, often expressed in terms of units (hours, number of people or completed actions).* In your logic model, outputs refer to the activities you will conduct and the people you hope to reach. **NOTE:** More than one OUTPUT is necessary to produce a final OUTCOME.	• Number of hours of professional development and number of teachers participating. • Units of Instruction submitted for peer review. • Assessment results and Grades.	
OUTCOMES *The results or impact of these activities or services, often expressed in terms of an increase in understanding, and improvements in desired behaviors or attitudes of participants.* In your logic model, outcomes refer to the short-term, mid-term, and long-term goals of your program. **NOTE:** A single OUTCOME is often the result of multiple OUTPUTS.	• Increased use of differentiated learning techniques. • Interdependence for common planning and assessment. • Demonstration by students of learning.	

The purpose of this worksheet is to help participants appreciate the difference between Outputs and Outcomes and how it takes multiple outputs to realize an outcome. I also use this worksheet to get participants to begin envisioning what they would like to achieve as leaders and the outputs they will need to plan for to achieve that outcome. As you review this worksheet, play particular attention to how outputs and outcomes are defined.

Outputs are the direct measurable products of a program's activities or services, often expressed in terms of units, such as hours, people or completed actions. This can be easily contextualized for education in that outputs for teachers are lesson plans, reports and amount of time spent for professional development.

Outcomes are the results of the combined activities, often expressed in terms of an increase in understanding and improvements in desired behaviors or attitudes. For example, an outcome we desire when offering professional development to teachers is an increase in confidence. The increase in confidence is the result of several outputs, one of which would be successfully using a new strategy they were introduced to, which would be measured by how students responded to the strategy.

> "NOT HOW MANY WORMS THE BIRD FEEDS ITS YOUNG, BUT HOW WELL THE FLEDGLING FLIES."
> – UNITED WAY OF AMERICA, 1999

This quote from United Way illustrates not only the difference between outputs and outcomes but the critical importance of connecting the two. What matters most is the importance (how well the young bird learns to fly), even though it might be easier to focus attention on an output (how many worms it feeds on) because that's easier to measure.

Collaboration is a Process

Like any system, the more points of contact there are, the more points of failure that need to be accounted for. The increased need for input is the most likely point of failure, as perceptions of observable data and expectations for outputs, both experience- and belief-driven, can vary greatly among team members[4]. Team members are also working under duress, in that they must invest a greater amount of time to achieve the outcome, which, if the collaboration is not seen as benefiting them, will be perceived as an additional duty obstructing their primary job responsibilities.

In the table below I demonstrate the difference between outputs and outcomes by providing an example of how they are placed within a system involving multiple inputs and processes. I believe outputs are the product of goals and/or professional inquiries. These products, though, are distilled through processes that require raw resources

---

[4] This will be discussed in greater detail when I introduce the Inference Ladder in Chapter 11 as a mechanism for team members to effectively harness disparity in perceptions to improve performance.

(inputs). Some of these processes can be quite complex with the inputs being quite difficult to acquire, such as *analyzing data* and *shared goal*.

The outcome, to *inform effectiveness of instruction*, may seem very straightforward on the surface, but when broken down, teams need to identify a shared interest in the area of practice they want to be informed on, as well as the data that will be used. In addition, analyzing data is a complex process that can leave many teachers feeling vulnerable and defensive. Effectively executing that process requires the following inputs: a high degree of trust, an appreciation for protocol and a strong facilitator. Therefore, if a team doesn't have the requisite amount of trust required to engage in protocol, then a team leader should first focus on building trust as their outcome and identify outputs that contribute to developing trust. The processes would be the activities that produce those outputs, and the inputs would be materials, attitudes, or contributions required to successfully facilitate those activities.

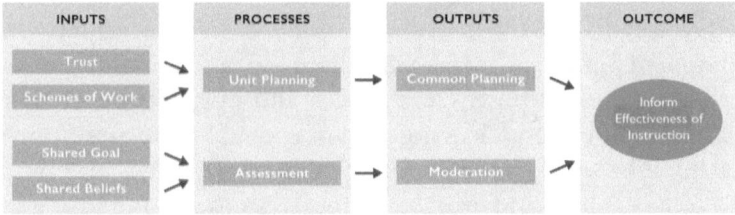
Teaching Teams

An often-overlooked input by senior leaders and team leaders is the common and understandable question, **what's in it for me**, which most educators will have at some point. The answer to this question will essentially determine if the team members and other essential stakeholders are invested in the collaborative venture they are expected to pursue. As a senior leader or a team leader, you may understand the problem that needs to be solved or the direction that the team must move in, but to successfully execute the processes, you need to ensure buy-in.

Another often-overlooked input by senior leaders is that the role of a team leader is understood. They assume that by taking on this challenge, the team leader can step into these roles and manage peers.

Those selected presumably have great organization skills, have good relationships with their peers and are respected. However, **when ascending to the team leader role, the dynamics of their peer relationship change, as well as their relationship with senior leaders.** The teacher-leader is now caught in between what are often two competing agendas.

If staff haven't bought into the school's expectations for the team, they will exert pressure on the team leader to push back. If senior leaders feel the team is underperforming, they will micromanage the team leader, disempowering them and forcing a reliance on senior leaders to mitigate conflict within the team. Negotiating between these two competing factions can be taxing and time-consuming; all told, the will to do anything transformative can be quickly diminished. **If the team leader is unable to align the interests of the team with the needs of the school, teams will focus on their primary work tasks and pursue transactional goals** within their realm of control and where their professional confidence is nested.

The Visioning Process and Alignment

Transcending *transactional collaboration* to achieve *transformational outcomes* begins with discussions that identify a team's core values and purpose. **Core values and purpose are often only implicitly understood, leaving a lot of room for interpretation and creating a breeding ground for conflict.** Core values and purpose need to be explicit, and artifacts of these values and purpose need to be constantly visible. Department, subject, and grade-level teams that take time at the beginning of each school year to reflect on and *document* their members' beliefs and values will find it much easier to build consensus on how to align the work of the team with the school's guiding statements and strategic goals. The process and practices teams choose to adopt can be unique to their team, but the goals they choose should reflect the school's values and reinforce its core purpose.

The importance of aligning with the school's core values and purpose is not just a matter of effective recruitment and ensuring cultural fit. Middle leaders need to ensure their teams plan each year with that purpose in mind and ensure those values are demonstrated in how their team executes its plans. The middle leadership team, introduced in Chapter 3, becomes the ideal starting point at the end of a school year for senior leaders to reflect on what the school has accomplished and where it needs to go. During this engagement, the vision of the school can be reinforced and the mission clarified.

Jim Collins, in a 1996 Harvard Business Review article famously stated:

> "COMPANIES THAT ENJOY ENDURING SUCCESS HAVE CORE VALUES AND A CORE PURPOSE THAT REMAINS FIXED WHILE THEIR BUSINESS STRATEGIES AND PRACTICES ENDLESSLY ADAPT TO A CHANGING WORLD."
>
> – BUILDING YOUR COMPANY'S VISION, JAMES C. COLLINS & JERRY I. PORRAS, HARVARD BUSINESS REVIEW, SEPT-OCT 1996 ISSUE

All schools have guiding statements that should include their vision and mission statements, but this doesn't mean that teams within the school shouldn't also engage in the same visioning process and devise their own statements of purpose. **To achieve alignment, teams need to articulate the school's guiding statements to account for their specific working context.** The articulation of the guiding statements is essentially reaffirming the core values and core purpose of the school to the team's own context. Rearticulating the guiding statements into a statement of purpose for the team empowers them to identify goals that are specific to their context and representative of the broader mission. In Chapter 9, I will provide detailed instructions for how to facilitate collaboratively drafting a team statement of purpose.

For educators, the school's guiding statements can often be vague and intangible. The team's articulation of the guiding statements not only ensures clarity of purpose but also alignment. If all teams can align with the school's guiding statements, it will be easier to bridge differences and collaborate based on mutual interests and shared goals. All teams, and their members, will now be stakeholders with vested interests in seeing the school achieve its mission. The individual teams will also have a greater chance of achieving their transformative goals because of the collaborative culture that has developed. A collaborative culture focused on outcomes looks and feels like this:

- Staff hallway and break room chatter will include constructive "gossip" about respective team challenges and "boasting" about progress;
- Teams talk about the work of other teams;
- Senior leadership periodically sit in, and are welcome, at team meetings;
- Team members look forward to the 45 minutes each week they get to spend with their team;
- Team members seek each other out to share successes and seek feedback on challenges; and
- Professional confidence increases.

The school will also have a greater chance of leveraging the work of its teams to achieve transformative outcomes. Teams that are given a say in any initiative that may affect their work, especially regarding the resources or additional support they may require, will become invested in that initiative and be more resilient during the implementation phase.

A secondary subject leader, put it this way: "In my personal experience, I find that teachers are often on board to promote the school's objectives, but what we lack is clarity and consistency in the message. We want to help build and vocalize these objectives to the wider school community, but often feel frustrated because we don't have a clear understanding of what these objectives are."

If there is a sense that the senior leaders' actions do not reflect stated values and serve the core purpose of the school, then any interpretation of the vision can seem superficial. Teams will default to setting goals that are the direct and measurable products of their work: transactional goals. Transactional goals require the least amount of investment in time and relationships to agree upon, and are the easiest to get approval for, such as planning units of instruction or identifying targets defined by time, cost, or scores. **Transactional goals often fall short of increasing understanding or improving desired behaviors or attitudes**; in other words, they fall short of achieving transformational outcomes.

Additionally, schools that want to rearticulate or draft new guiding statements as an exercise for accreditation, to elevate their profile in the market, to reinvigorate the community, to mask problems within the community, or as a means to initiate undesired change will fail to motivate teams to achieve transformational outcomes. The snowball effect from poorly supported and communicated guiding statements is immense, as it leads to a superficial sense of purpose that will discourage teams from aligning with the stated values and purpose of the school. Teams will then default to working solely for the purpose of executing their primary responsibilities. **The problem in many cases are not the guiding statements, but senior leadership's inability to measure the school's performance against the guiding statements and align staff with the stated values and purpose of the school.**

An easy way to diagnose if your school or team has fallen prey to a superficial sense of purpose is to:

1. List what you are passionate about.
2. List what your school's greatest strengths or differentiators are.
3. List three reasons why parents choose your school.
4. List three reasons why teachers apply to your school.
5. Compare your lists to the school's vision, mission, and strategic goals. Do they align?

What level of disparity have you noticed between your list and what the school states as its values (what it is passionate about; its vision) and why people choose to attend or work (the core purpose) at your school? Now, try to imagine how that disparity can grow as middle management and staff are further removed from the operational drivers of the school. By operational drivers, I mean having buy-in related to decisions for strategic objectives, recruitment, or professional development.

The proverbial snowball quickly builds as our performance management and recruitment practices fail to reinforce the values and core purpose of the school. Staff will quickly retreat to the familiar instead of exploring the unknown. Staff at all levels are hired to do a job, and they want to do the job to the best of their ability. However, **if you need staff to step outside their comfort zone and take on new challenges, they will need to have a shared belief about that purpose, which requires an understanding of the expectations for their role and buy-in to define the outcome.** There may be initial resistance to the expectations being placed on them or disparity in terms of how the outcome is defined, but acceptance and adjusting for that disparity is good. The difference in how the team's purpose is perceived and the desired outcome is defined, and, more important, the acceptance of those differences, is what leads to achieving transformational outcomes.

The snowball effect, however, does not necessarily mean that the school or its teams will be unable to educate students. Educators, including non-academic staff, are incredibly passionate about their work and will not allow it to be devalued by ambiguous objectives. The resilience of educators, and the fact that many tend to be pragmatic, is ultimately the reason why teams never evolve beyond transactional collaboration. Leaders and teachers will persevere in the face of ambiguity and focus on their primary objectives. Focusing solely on individual objectives, and not those set by the school or team, ultimately leaves departments, teams, and even individual staff isolated, effectively working in silos. Teamwork will be limited to what they can control. Attention will focus on achieving outputs and not on how work can harmonize and align with other teams to produce transformative outcomes.

Similar to how the school's guiding statements need to be interpreted at all levels across the school, outcomes also need to be differentiated at each level in the school. Boards and senior leadership need to be accountable for long-term outcomes, those that are evaluated over five to ten years. Middle leaders need to be accountable for outcomes that can be evaluated over a three-year period. The scope and scale of the goals that culminate in those outcomes being evidenced vary greatly, and therefore the authority and resources delegated to the various levels of leadership need to be commensurate and explicit. By explicitly defining the authority and resources delegated to middle leaders, as well as clearly defining their role and expectations, boundaries for their sandbox are set. Sandboxes, which are the subject of the next chapter, are the building blocks of transformative change.

CHAPTER 5

THE SANDBOX

Who doesn't love seeing kids play in a sandbox? Take this picture, for instance. Take a minute to observe what is going on in this picture.

I see 4 distinct activities taking place in the same space, of which 3 are collaborative. Resources are being cooperatively shared. I see looks of curiosity, smiles and sand sculptures being made.

This is the proverbial sandbox that I hope your teams can create and play in. They are defined by purpose and when properly established, you should be able to make the same observations as the first image: Networked collaboration, cooperative resource sharing, curiosity, positive relationships and tangible products being created.

Schools that empower their middle leaders to take ownership of their teams will demonstrate these six characteristics:

1. Differentiate the expectations for each leader (Chapter 1);
2. Select leaders that are "stage appropriate" and have shared values with the community (Chapter 2);
3. Provide a platform for middle leaders to share resources and best practices and communicate with senior leaders (Chapter 3);
4. Evaluate leaders on outcomes (Chapter 4);
5. Clarify the role, expectations, and available resources (Chapter 5); and
6. Allocate time for planning and development (Chapter 6).

In this chapter, we will explore the role senior leaders play to ensure middle leaders have clarity of purpose and appropriate resourcing to seed their success. Teacher leaders, coordinators, department heads, and vice-principals are the true change agents in schools and will be the most effective tool in ensuring transformative and sustained change. To achieve transformative outcomes, we not only need their buy-in, but we also need to empower them by defining and equipping the *sandbox* within which they play.

In corporate IT parlance, sandboxes are insulated testing grounds that allow programmers to develop and test applications before releasing them into the real world. The sandbox begins as a "clean room," void of any possible contaminants, but it ultimately is intended to be a simulation of the operating environment the applications will be used in. Sandboxes in this way have several iterations, with the intent of progressively getting closer and closer to real-world operations, with integration, acceptance, and alpha and beta tests. It is because of this iterative progression that sandboxes are not silos. Applications have proven ready for release because there has already been a significant amount of interaction between the applications and the world that awaits them.

In 2004–05, a conspiracy theory around the Google search algorithms erupted: the *Google Sandbox Theory*. Developers who had up to this point made a lot of money from search engine optimization (SEO), and felt they had "gamed" the system, employed all their best practices but weren't finding their sites in the top search results any longer. In some cases, they weren't finding their sites in any results for relevant search terms. The most likely reason is that before Google promotes websites, they "sandbox" them for an undefined period to ensure the content is relevant to the searches. In one respect, the websites are "live," listed, and accessible, but before Google promotes them in searches, according to the developers' design, the search engine wants to study how the world interacts with the website.

Imagine sandboxing a new lesson planning tool, learning management system, assessment strategy, or even communication tools for a sample of parents. While one group is trialing the tool or strategy, the rest of the community can be kept informed and prepare for its eventual release. During this same time, someone on the same team is assigned with the task of observing how teachers, students and parents are responding to the new strategy or communication tool. Unfortunately, too many schools rush into implementing new strategies or tools without sandboxing them first; resulting in poor implementation, frustrated staff and in most cases failure to realize the intended outcome.

The corporate world over the past twenty years, beyond IT, has also embraced sandboxes for organizational development. Schools, to a small degree, also use sandboxes; they just don't know it. The sandbox effect in schools is often a result of high-functioning teams insulating themselves from a culture of complacency. These sandboxes, unfortunately, prevent the propagation of good practice, as they lack the input and support of key stakeholders, and there are no connections across the school, like a middle leadership team. Performance evaluation, interdisciplinary teams, leadership succession, budgeting, master planning, and communication strategies are examples that have been successfully sandboxed and helped organizations achieve transformative change.

The sandbox, though, can get quite messy. Contaminants can fester in a sandbox that is not churned and cleared properly. Before letting my children play in any sandbox, I like to run my hand through the sand to ensure there is nothing sharp or unhygienic. In a school context, something sharp may be a competing initiative, and something unhygienic could be a team member's attitude toward an initiative.

Senior leaders, in their rush to introduce new ideas to staff, fail to appreciate how new ideas and initiatives will negatively influence existing staff capacity, regardless of whether the ideas are well received. Ideas can quickly evolve into initiatives that are introduced (imposed) on teams without clearing the sandbox. Even if new initiatives are properly planned and buy-in appropriately sought, but the sandbox isn't cleared, then the initiative is vulnerable to contamination. So, ensuring our middle leaders have a clean sandbox to play in is incredibly important, but equally important is knowing what and who are in the sandbox before anything new starts to be built in it.

Building the Sandbox

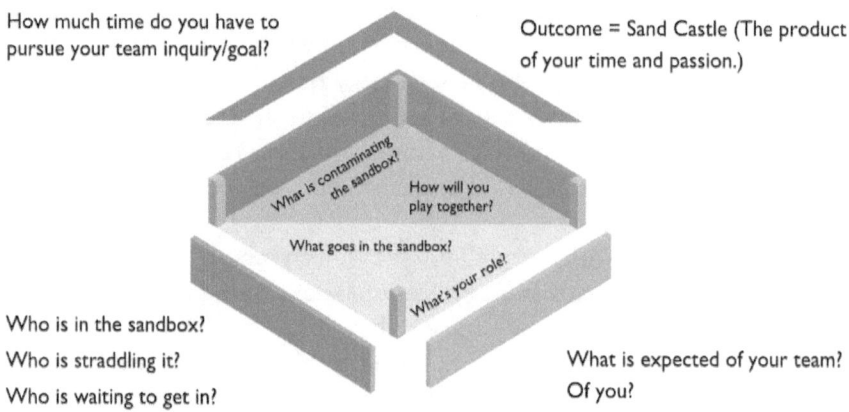

How much time do you have to pursue your team inquiry/goal?

Outcome = Sand Castle (The product of your time and passion.)

Who is in the sandbox?
Who is straddling it?
Who is waiting to get in?

What is expected of your team?
Of you?

A sandbox requires boundaries and rules, not just to keep the sand in, but also to prevent the sandbox from getting too busy or dirty. The walls of the sandbox are the rules that govern what goes in and what comes out. The sandbox is a finite space, which limits the scale of what a team wants to achieve (sand), the resources at the team's disposal (pales and shovels), and number of people the sandbox can accommodate. Like any play area, the sandbox requires regular cleaning and maintenance. We need to protect the sand and ensure that after each play session, we properly churn and clean it.

Before we throw in new initiatives or change the team composition, let us assess the current state of a team's sandbox to verify the team:

STAGE	Can the team's current stage of development accommodate the initiative? Will adding something new cause the team to regress?
CULTURE	What behaviors demonstrate those values?
CAPACITY	How does this align with the work culture you are seeking?

To strengthen the walls of the sandbox, we need to ensure stability by reassuring middle leaders their role is secure beyond one year. Providing middle leaders with a three-year horizon ensures there is more space for planning, coordination, and professional development; to realize the full impact of these activities in one year is impossible. With more time and ample support, middle leaders will settle into their role and devise strategies and practices to utilize resources and people more effectively.

To empower middle leaders, we also need to provide them a safety net for mistakes and space for reflection. In a proper sandboxed environment, failure within the team becomes a growth opportunity, not demoralizing breakroom whispers. As we reflect on the journey of middle leaders to achieve transformational collaborative change within their team and school, we need to respect the time and investment that is necessary to complete that journey. Transformative change is not achieved in a year; we need effective middle leaders to think of their role in terms of multi-year horizons.

Since transformative outcomes take three to five years to achieve, we can't risk losing effective middle leaders amid change. When I speak with middle leaders that are planning to leave a school, they focus on transactional tasks to ensure closure when they leave. This focus on transactional tasks is effectively an abandonment of the transformational outcome.

Unfortunately, their departure alters the sandbox environment, the experience they accrued is potentially lost, and the middle leader stepping into their position needs time to align themselves with the team and change initiative. This last aspect of alignment, ensuring the new middle leader is bought into and aligned with an ongoing change initiative, is precisely why a multi-stakeholder approach to recruitment is so important, as it will take several senior leaders to understand the current state of change and who is needed to see change through.

Educators are incredibly efficacious; if their sandbox is not properly defined, they will define it themselves, and commit to transactional outputs within their control. Regardless of whether they have been in the role for three years or are just stepping into the role in the midst of change, middle leaders will break senior leaders' expectations down into practical and achievable chunks, the culmination of which seldom matches the expectations of the senior leaders. Senior leaders, for this reason, need to ensure that people essential to the success of an initiative understand the expectations explicitly and commit to the full duration of the initiative.

Establishing a Sandbox for a Year 6-8 PLC Team

With the boundaries of the sandbox established, it is important that we insulate it from contaminants, which can vary from not properly bringing closure to past initiatives to members of the community who are vehemently opposed to change. Those working within the sandbox need to be champions for change, stakeholders that the change will not only benefit directly, but will actively advocate for it when the time is right. Stakeholder management is critical to achieving change in an organization. My beliefs and experiences managing stakeholders in large organizations has been influenced by Joel A. Barker's book, *Future Edge: Discovering the New Paradigms of Success*. Barker broke stakeholders down into five groups, split along these percentages, **10-20-40-20-10**. This is not a hard-and-fast rule about how stakeholders break down in every organization or community, but I have yet to visit a school where it deviates much. These proportions are also, coincidentally, found in marketing, management, and professional learning literature, and I have relabeled the groupings to reflect how they effect change:

10% - CHAMPIONS	- Staff who are hungry to effect change, no matter the costs.
20% - CHEERLEADERS	- Staff who want change but are wary of the costs.
40% - FENCE SITTERS	- Staff who want to see the benefits of change before they adopt it.
20% - NAYSAYERS	- Staff who predict gloom and doom and will advocate against change.
10% - AGGRESSORS	- Staff who are completely closed to the idea of change and will fight it.

In marketing terms, the first 30% are the early adopters, with the 40% being the mass market that identifies with your brand and needs time to run through the current product cycle. In the field of professional learning, several speakers, including myself, know we go into every event expecting that 30% of the people are hungry to hear what we have to say, 30% wish they didn't have to be there, and the other 40% open to our ideas, but want explicit guidance on how to implement ideas.

For the sandbox to be free of contaminants, we need to ensure it is only filled with the first 30% of stakeholders and insulated from the last 30%. The middle 40% should be invited to be active observers. I do not advocate for censoring the last 30%, but I do feel they should be left alone, with no expectations to have their time or attention distracted by what is happening in that sandbox. Ultimately, what happens when this strategy is successfully implemented is that observers will engage with champions to better understand their experience and will begin to find ways they can apply what they have learned to suit their own context. As the wave of momentum builds, the naysayers and aggressors become self-censored and ultimately feel uncomfortable in the community and either leave it or are asked to leave. This process of turnover, though, can take anywhere from one to ten years, hence why it is so important to ensure we have senior leaders committed to change for that period of time.

I want to share with you the journey of a middle leader, Alexa, and how, by defining her sandbox, she was able to free herself to pursue transformative outcomes with champions and cheerleaders. The school Alexa worked at was similar to many other schools I have helped to become outcome-focused. Alexa was part of the champions demographic, eager to effect change, the change in this case being the establishment of learning communities across the school (effectively one of the many variations of the PLC concept). Her role was the Year-6-to-8[5] middle school (MS) learning community leader.

This MS learning community had a core group of twelve teachers who taught most of the middle school classes and also regularly interacted in the staff room, which had always been the site for collaborative exchanges. The teachers were spread across several subject discipline areas. Two of the twelve MS core teachers had their own specialist spaces (science and design technology labs) and rarely came to sit with the rest of the group. One of those teachers had not seemed to buy in to the collaboration concept and one of them was new, lacking any background information, so there was effectively a core group of ten.

Because of the increasingly diverse population of the school, more teachers were needed to fill the teaching schedule, enlarging the MS learning community as a result. The other teachers in this community were spread out between the year 9–11 learning community and the year 12–13 learning community. The entire MS team was about twenty-six teachers, including teachers who primarily taught in the IB or IGCSE and only came down to teach MS for one or two periods. As a result, these teachers weren't ever in the staff room and were for the most part disconnected from the MS community. They were not in a space to see the value in a collaborative and integrated approach to curriculum development.

Alexa began the year, 2017, prepared to build on curricular initiatives she had championed the year before as the Professional Development (PD) Coordinator for the whole school. Her

---

[5] For the purpose of this case, I am using the British system for grade levels, which distinguishes age levels by the term year and not grade; year 1 is equivalent to the North American level of kindergarten, therefore there are 13 year levels.

expectations were an extension of the inquiry-based learning program I introduced when she was the PD Coordinator. The outcome she sought was for the Year 6–8 MS learning community to develop a curriculum that was collaboratively designed and included integrated end-of-unit projects. The desired outcome was for students to make links between subject areas and be invigorated with the thought of preparing projects that drew from various subject areas. Student learning would increase in breadth and depth. Teachers would come out of their isolated subject areas and divisions to work together without needing planned meeting times.

Prior to the PD Coordinator role, in 2015, Alexa was the Year-6 team leader. So, between 2015 and 2017, Alexa served in three different middle leadership roles. Each team she oversaw had significant overlap, so she had a core group of followers. Even as a PD Coordinator, which was part-time, she still met with the Year-6 team on curricular initiatives they had begun in 2015. Additionally, in this school, the goals and expectations for middle leaders changed from year to year, evidenced in Alexa serving in so many roles. As a year-level leader, she focused intensely on common planning and supporting team members. As a PD Coordinator, she was asked to plan schoolwide PD initiatives and begin seeding the development of learning communities.

In each role, despite the initiatives she was overseeing requiring multi-year planning, her planning capabilities were limited to a one-year window. This occurs because all the variables necessary to achieve the outcome are staffed, budgeted for, and calendared year to year. Middle leaders plan based on what they know. When looking back, this approach seems rational. But for those looking forward, the activities and expectations are ambiguous. There is no data on the efficacy of their contributions. Furthermore, *we don't know what we don't know*; therefore, as PD Coordinator and a key stakeholder in the learning community initiative, much of her time was spent selling the initiative to colleagues.

The learning community initiative was an obstacle to other work that teachers would be able to derive more immediate gratification from. By not sandboxing the learning community initiative, Alexa had to attend to a larger number of stakeholder needs and competing interests (contaminants). Each team had varying degrees of buy-in and competing priorities and were in different stages of development, thus requiring varying degrees and types of support. As a PD Coordinator, her scope and capacity were limited. Her limited planning window became much smaller because of all the time and resources that got spent dealing with things she didn't know.

Upon assuming the role of learning leader, Alexa was incredibly frustrated, as she found her meetings being hijacked by other school leader announcements and general lack of buy-in from a majority of community members. All these members also belonged to other teams and other learning communities, impeding her ability to work with all members and ensure their interests aligned. In fact, she was only able to meet with the whole learning community six times per year for two hours at a time.

Alexa was effectively limited to her core group of ten and she felt constrained and was quickly losing hope of achieving her goal set for that year. Unfortunately, her ambitions exceeded the capacity of her sandbox. To Alexa, the dilemma she faced was to either abandon curriculum initiative she had begun as a Year-6 team leader and worked very hard to support as a PD Coordinator, or to press forward with the outcome limited to her core team, effectively siloed. A significant obstacle for Alexa was that she was living in the moment, not stepping back and assessing her situation or defining her sandbox.

Let's first reflect on her goal: *The Year 6–8 MS learning community will develop a curriculum that is collaboratively designed and includes integrated end-of-unit projects.* To achieve this goal, I advised her to step back and make explicit why this goal was important. Often, the core purpose of a goal is not made explicit. In many cases this is because team leaders don't want to specifically address sensitive issues or because they want to make sure the goal sounds interesting for everyone. To ensure the core purpose was made explicit, I asked her to develop a driving (focus) question, something that would focus her on the core purpose. Her initial focus question was this: *How can I help facilitate a cultural shift in the secondary teachers to help them become increasingly more collaborative, specifically for resistant teachers and between different curriculum areas?* This question would be revised, but it was a good starting point, mainly because we now knew why this was important to Alexa.

With a focus question established, she could begin to have more direct and focused dialog with team members to see if they also desired to achieve this core purpose; essentially confirm if they wanted to play in the sandbox. From what we know thus far, we can assume the entire learning community of twenty-six teachers did not. As we began to address the focus question, it became clear that it was far too large in scope for what authority she had. It is not up to a single individual to cause a culture shift, let alone to expect it within a year. That is putting way too much pressure on one person.

Furthermore, when we simplified the focus question, what we were really seeking was interdisciplinary collaboration. The entire community of twenty-six teachers was only scheduled to meet six times per year, whereas the core team of ten regularly met in the staff room. Lastly, this core team of ten teachers did share an interest in achieving the core purpose. At this stage, we 1) made explicit the core purpose (scope of the sandbox), 2) identified team members that had a shared interest (who would play in the sandbox), and 3) began to clarify Alexa's authority.

Now we needed to redefine her role in the sandbox and agreed on this: She would need to stop focusing on the administrative tasks for most of her day and focus on curriculum. She would need to help teachers find links between their subject areas and then help them find times to meet in hopes that they could work together. She would need to have opportunities to celebrate successes between teams and let others, who were unsure of the challenges or were skeptics, understand the vision for the learning community curriculum. She also wanted to try to observe some teaching to see how the concept was addressed during lessons and to see what links the students were making. What she had now were tangible and actionable responsibilities.

Once Alexa and I had completed a couple coaching sessions, we redrafted her focus question: How can I facilitate the development of our curriculum realignment within the Year 6–8 middle school learning community in order to encourage greater subject integration and teacher collaboration? For some this may still seem lofty, but for Alexa it was liberating.

Setting Middle Leaders Up for Success

Regardless of if the middle leader has a full-time teaching role, they should still have their job description evaluated and amended annually to clearly define the leadership responsibilities they are assuming, as well as the expectations and resources that come with those responsibilities. If the role is clearly defined and the expectations laid out and agreed to, then we can secure and clean their sandbox. A secure sandbox effectively mitigates the problem of time, or more to the point, helps middle leaders better understand how to use their time.

The time problem is more pronounced for middle leaders that have too much going on in their sandbox, not to mention still teaching in a classroom. For those middle leaders who are not in the classroom, but are still hindered by the time problem, it is most likely because they are taking on too many initiatives and/or micromanaging work across multiple sandboxes. Senior leaders need to acknowledge that good leadership isn't just something someone does. Those who can effectively navigate space and time demonstrate good leadership. Unfortunately, these are two variables that middle leaders have very little power to control.

Alexa's case is also excellent for demonstrating the different strategies, experience, and leadership skills needed in each leadership role. Year-level and subject leaders require much different leadership skills than coordinators. The learning leader role in this case is effectively a hybrid of both. Year-level and subject leaders have smaller teams to oversee; therefore, they need to explore subject matter much more deeply, while learning at the same time. Coordinators don't necessarily have a team, but they are expected to distil knowledge across teams and support learning, which requires better interpersonal skills. In the next chapter, we will begin to explore how to develop leadership capacity to support the multi-dimensional middle leader.

CHAPTER 6

BUILDING MIDDLE LEADERSHIP CAPACITY

Collaboration Requires Leadership

> "COLLABORATION IS NOT ALWAYS A CONCEPT THAT IS GREETED WITH OPEN ARMS. EDUCATORS WHO HAVE HAD SUCCESS WORKING IN ISOLATION MAY VIEW THIS PROCESS AS AN INVASION OF THEIR PEDAGOGY AND A WASTE OF TIME.
>
> THE KEY TO STRONG COLLABORATION IS RECOGNIZING THAT A STUDENT SHOULDN'T BE THE RESPONSIBILITY OF ONLY ONE TEACHER, BUT OF ALL TEACHERS."
>
> – JASON PEREZ, HEAD PRINCIPAL AT HERITAGE TRAILS ELEMENTARY, "TAKING THE DOORS OFF THE CLASSROOM THROUGH COLLABORATION," BLOG POST DATED JANUARY 7TH, 2015

The simplest form of collaboration, and style of leadership for that matter, is one-to-one. Unfortunately, though, two is not the most effective team size. Research on teams and collaboration indicates that the most effective team size is between five and ten members. However, the larger the team, the more likely the team will suffer from increased relationship conflict, process and coordination delays, and social loafing. But, if the team size is too small—say, less than four—the team suffers from lack of perspective.

MICHAEL R. IANNINI

Many teaching teams average about five to six people, and, in my opinion, this is about as big of a team a middle leader can achieve transformative outcomes with. My reasoning for this belief is largely due to the actual authority middle leaders are given. Many middle leaders have no formal authority, their authority is largely a result of team members trusting them. To be fair, size shouldn't matter as much as the task before the team and the team leader's capacity to lead.

For the sake of argument and accepting that how schools organize staff probably won't change any time soon, this chapter will assume your middle leader is planning and coordinating the work for a team of five people. Coordinating the work of five people is a large undertaking when you are also teaching five classes or coordinating curriculum or activities across multiple teams.

Regardless of the size of the team, though, anyone that cares about improving teaching and learning should always be open to collaboration, and more importantly working through the logistics of developing a transformative collaborative team culture. Vicki Vescio's paper, *A Review of Research on the Impact of Professional Learning Communities on Teaching Practice and Student Learning*, evidences the positive correlation between teacher collaboration and student learning. There is ample research, and anecdotal experience, which should be reason enough to put aside fears of "invasion of pedagogy" or of being evaluated. If we hold each other accountable for the success of all students, not just our own, then collaboration is not only necessary, but should be our primary responsibility.

Collaboration, though, is not spontaneous, it requires effective leadership and team member buy-in. Leadership in this case is a loaded term; as I explained in Chapter 1, the needs of each team vary, especially in terms of what form of leadership they will respond most positively to. Therefore, once the team leader has been identified, the next step is to determine what training and resources they will need to succeed. Leadership training in and of itself only creates awareness of what is expected of a leader and provides additional lenses through which leaders should view their work.

An example of a critical failure in teams and in leadership training to address that failure, as evidenced in a 1995 study by Linda A. Hill, is when a leader focuses their attention on an individual team member, as opposed to fostering relationships between team members. No leadership program that I have reviewed or participated in instructs middle leaders on how to get team members with disparate values, beliefs, and practices to collaborate.

There is a lot of literature on building effective teams, navigating difficult conversations, and collaborating within teams, but they all ignore the fact that middle leaders don't get to choose their team, nor do they have authority to remove team members that do not buy in to the purpose of the team. Therefore, once the middle leaders have been oriented with the level of awareness and expectations related to their role, they need to invest an inordinate amount of time to transition from being a team leader to the leader of a team. The leader of a team is not at the center and supervising each team member's work, but is tangled in a web of interdependent interactions.

Building Middle Leadership Capacity

In this chapter, I will explore how to identify what a middle leader needs to learn, continue to make the argument for why middle leaders need more time set aside to build their leadership capacity, and the role failure plays in developing great leaders. First, though, let me define "building capacity," as this is not a common educational term, especially among middle leaders. The best definition I have found for building capacity as it relates to my work with schools comes from a paper by Bill Hoag and a book by Linda Lambert.

The general definition that I subscribe to, as written by Bill Hoag, is:

> "**BUILDING LEADERSHIP CAPACITY** IS A PROCESS THAT STARTS WITH UNDERSTANDING THE CONCEPT OF **LEADERSHIP CAPACITY**, DEFINING THE EXPECTATIONS OF **LEADERSHIP** WITHIN YOUR PARTICULAR ORGANIZATION, AND THEN **BUILDING** INTENTIONAL, IMPLEMENTABLE STEPS THAT HELP **LEADERS** ASSESS AND DEVELOP THEIR ABILITY TO BE A **LEADER**."

MICHAEL R. IANNINI

The concept of leadership capacity has been explored thoroughly in the preceding chapters, but it is the strategy of the sandbox that makes the term tangible. The sandbox ensures the expectations and roles are explicitly defined. The sandbox also determines the requisite leadership capacity needed to achieve the desired outcome, which in turn should assist senior leaders in providing adequate support to build leadership capacity.

Support is more than just skill development, and senior leaders cannot outsource capacity building to training programs or achieve it with a few motivational anecdotes about their time in the trenches. According to Bill Hoag:

> "LEADERSHIP CAPACITY IS MORE THAN SIMPLY SKILL DEVELOPMENT; IT IS ABOUT PERFORMANCE, GROWTH, TRANSFORMATION, AND CHANGE.... GREAT LEADERS NOT ONLY UNDERSTAND HOW TO ENGAGE AND INSPIRE THEIR TEAMS TO GET THE BEST RESULTS—THEY UNDERSTAND THE NEED TO CREATE PARTICIPATORY AND COLLABORATIVE PROCESSES THAT DEVELOP THE ABILITIES OF THE NEXT GENERATION OF LEADERS."
>
> – BUILDING LEADERSHIP CAPACITY
> **BY BILL HOAG AND ASSOCIATES**

Linda Lambert's book, *Building Leadership Capacity in Schools*, helps to contextualize the process of "understanding the concept of leadership capacity," and her definition goes further by providing rich detail as to how to assess full capacity:

> "LEADERSHIP IS ABOUT LEARNING TOGETHER AND CONSTRUCTING MEANING AND KNOWLEDGE COLLECTIVELY AND COLLABORATIVELY. IT INVOLVES OPPORTUNITIES TO SURFACE AND MEDIATE PERCEPTIONS, VALUES, BELIEFS, INFORMATION, AND ASSUMPTIONS THROUGH CONTINUING CONVERSATIONS; TO INQUIRE ABOUT AND GENERATE IDEAS TOGETHER; TO SEEK TO REFLECT UPON AND MAKE SENSE OF WORK IN THE LIGHT OF SHARED BELIEFS AND NEW INFORMATION; AND TO CREATE ACTIONS THAT GROW OUT OF THESE NEW UNDERSTANDINGS."

Lambert makes an important point in the opening chapter of her book, "We generally consider leadership to be synonymous with a person in a position of formal authority... When we equate "leadership" with "leader," we are immersed in "trait theory": If only a leader possessed these certain traits, we would have good leadership... Although leaders do perform acts of leadership, a separation of the concepts can allow us to re-conceptualize leadership itself."

This point by Lambert further illustrates the problem of labels that are subject to different interpretations, similar to my examples for defining professionalism and collaboration. We can't expect people to lead unless we explicitly define and get buy-in for the values, beliefs, and expectations that will be the basis for how we define that label. With a commonly understood definition of leadership, relative to the needs of the school, senior leaders will have a better understanding of how to build their middle leaders' leadership capacity.

Here is a quote from a working group of senior leaders I moderated that was convened due to the growing interest in professionally developing middle leaders:

> "SCHOOLS NEED TO PROVIDE RESOURCES AND STRUCTURE THAT GUIDE MIDDLE LEADERS TOWARD AN OUTCOME THAT ALIGNS THEIR TEAM WITH THE NEEDS OF THE SCHOOL."

This interest has grown due to various challenges schools face: retention, recruitment, opportunity costs, PLCs, and encouraging leaders throughout the school to take more ownership of the school's performance. The members of this working group all agreed that their middle leaders were often asked to take on roles without a clear understanding of what was expected of them, and were seldom given sufficient training or tools to effectively lead their peers. As middle leaders are often on the front line themselves, they don't feel empowered as leaders and do not want to strain relationships with colleagues. The senior leaders in this working group agreed that operating in this type of environment can be stressful and, primarily for that reason, they were often called upon to resolve conflict among team members.

The objectives for developing the leadership capacity of middle leaders should be to:

1. Free senior leaders to focus on strategic objectives;
2. Capacity-build middle leaders to independently pursue team objectives aligned with the school; and
3. Instill trust and confidence that, regardless of the outcome, the work of middle leaders still contributes to the success of the school.

Plan on Working a Lot Harder Than You Ever Have

Middle leaders that are (1) bought into the expectations that are being placed on them and (2) have a clear understanding of the outcome they are being asked to contribute to should expect to work 2-3 hours more per week than they may be assuming. To turn outputs into outcomes requires a great amount of energy and time, neither of which middle leaders can expect to be remunerated nor given a single ounce of praise for.

The process to take a complacent team from a checklist approach to its work to a transformational collaborative team that challenges how things are done and works interdependently is a long and often thankless road. Very few activities and tools that I introduce, or that are recommended by any expert for that matter, can be fit into your normal work routine. These tools and activities require a deep level of consideration of the members that are participating in this process, confidence in the team leader's ability to achieve the outcome expected of the team, time to focus exclusively on the desired outcome, and a strong resolve to see through myriad conflicts.

A problem that is consistently woven through this book is a lack of time. When I introduced the Silo Dilemma, time was one of two problems that drove teams to be complacent; the other theme, which I will address now, is that of leadership development. The first problem is transparent and openly lamented. Leadership development is not so openly discussed.

Unfortunately for many schools, regardless of if middle leaders are bought in to the expectations being set and clearly understand those expectations, senior leaders still fail to provide them these two critical types of support: time and training. Middle leaders are left to scrape together time from the remnants of periods and breaks that they use to covet to catch up with colleagues. Learning on the job takes up additional time, strains collegial relationships, and undermines team member confidence in the team leader.

It is very likely that any team, as it is composed today, is not prepared to achieve any new outcome set for them. They will need time to understand the desired outcome, align their values and beliefs relative to that outcome, and assess how the desired outcome will impact curricular practices and students. In fact, the team leader may need to shelve their goals completely and allow the team to define how they will achieve the outcomes set by the senior leaders.

The team leader needs to see their role as long-term, at least three years. During this time, how will the team leader build and support the culture fit for the desired outcome? What skills and resources will the team leader need to guide their team toward the desired outcome? How should the team leader scaffold the activities that produce the necessary outputs over the three-year period? What changes in the team can the team leader prepare for and be proactive in facilitating? The answers to these questions address the gap between what the team leader is capable of doing now and the additional time in learning and leading they will need to invest to develop the necessary capacity to achieve the desired outcome.

Here are some examples of how answers to these questions form the outline of a training needs analysis:

QUESTION:

During this time, how will the team leader ensure cultural fit for the desired outcome?

ANSWER:

The following is an example of a desired outcome: *regular and unprovoked demonstrations of staff taking responsibility for the learning of all students by engaging in collaborative activities that surface questions about practice, inquire about and generate ideas related to those questions, make sense of work in the light of new information, and create actions that grow out of these new understandings.*

To realize this outcome, we need to make the values, beliefs, and behaviors that support this outcome explicit. We next need to determine which of the values, beliefs, and behaviors are currently observable in the day-to-day work of staff and which ones need to be reinforced and regularly assessed to ensure they become part of the way staff work.

REQUIRED CAPACITY:

The team leader needs awareness of how teams develop and familiarity with Tuckman's Stages (Forming, Storming, Norming, Performing, and Adjourning).[6] Specifically, the activities associated with the Forming Stage would be the best place to start. At the beginning of the school year, the team leader, in addition to clarifying roles and expectations, should facilitate three discussions:

1. To realize the answer for the desired outcome, define cultural fitness (Chapter 2);

2. Build consensus for the team's core purpose and align it with the desired outcome (Chapter 9); and

3. Surface and make explicit the values, beliefs, and behaviors that team members need to demonstrate and have at the core of their work. One of the most important products that will result from this discussion will be a team's group norms, also known as a social contract or norms of behavior (Chapter 8).

QUESTION:

What skills and resources will the team leader need to guide their team toward the desired outcome?

ANSWER:

The team will need time set aside to understand, plan, and engage in activities specific to the desired outcome. This is time in addition to the administrative matters they already attend to. The team needs to understand how to effectively use this time for only this purpose and facilitate discussions and activities related only to achieving the desired outcome.

---

6 Each stage is defined in Chapter 7.

REQUIRED CAPACITY:
- The team leader needs to be able to effectively manage meetings by making sure the purpose of each meeting is clear, team members arrive prepared, and meetings end in actions that support the purpose and can be reviewed in subsequent meetings.
- The team leader needs to be able to harness conflict as a tool for developing deeper awareness.

QUESTION:
How should the team leader scaffold the activities that produce the necessary outputs over the three-year period?

ANSWER:
- The first year should be spent with the team using time purposefully set aside for pursuing the desired outcome on team-building activities, reviewing and debating research, learning to build consensus when there are disparate views, sharing best practice, engaging in common planning, and celebrating demonstrations of collaboration.
- The second-year team members should pair up and identify specific areas of inquiry related to their practice, review relevant research, observe each other, debrief actions that resulted from the research and observations, and celebrate actions that yielded positive results.
- The third year, the team should identify an area of inquiry aligned to a strategic goal of the school and be able to demonstrate collectively being accountable for the performance of all students.

REQUIRED CAPACITY:
- The team leader needs to be able to help team members identify effective professional inquiries and take iterative steps to addressing those inquiries.
- The team leader needs to monitor and evaluate each team member's ability to demonstrate actions that address the professional inquiry.

- The team leader needs to be able to provide evaluative feedback to team members.

QUESTION:

What changes in the team can the team leader prepare for and be proactive in facilitating?

ANSWER:

Team member turnover is inevitable and discussions with team members and senior leaders early on can help to identify potential turnover in the team. Turnover should be viewed as healthy, as it may be someone getting a promotion or an opportunity to introduce a different perspective or a new skill set to the team.

Additionally, in the next three years, what governance activities and strategic objectives can we foresee that will impact the work of the team or any of its members, such as accreditation or changes in curriculum?

REQUIRED CAPACITY:

The team leader needs to be able to manage and understand the larger picture before they commit to long-term planning. To achieve this, the team leader needs regular interaction with senior leaders and buy-in to team member recruitment and strategic objectives that impact the team.

To demonstrate the required capacity to achieve the example of the desired outcome, middle leaders need to be able to achieve the following:

1. Ensure a shared understanding and beliefs about the desired outcome,
2. Build consensus on team values and core purpose, aligned with the desired outcome,
3. Make time to plan, coordinate, and debrief team activities,
4. Be aware of the work and progress of other teams, and
5. Build and support interdependencies within & around the team.

These points, in addition to defining the scope and scale of capacity that the middle leader is expected to fulfil, provide evaluative measures assessing the middle leader's development. For example, how aware is the middle leader of the progress other teams are making? Once the capacity requirements and evaluative measures are determined, appropriate development activities can be identified.

Capacity-Building Strategies

To develop a middle leader's capacity, schools have several strategies they can use. Renee Rehfeldt, one of the most experienced PD Coordinators I have met and worked with, defined the four strategies I list below to categorize the numerous PD offerings available to staff [7]:

INTERNAL PROFESSIONAL LEARNING	Teacher to teacher or staff to staff; conducted by the school for the school staff and guided by the school's needs, i.e., PLCs, observations, book clubs, visiting consultant workshops (in-service PD) and mentoring.
NETWORK PROFESSIONAL LEARNING	School to school (or multiple schools); organized by schools for schools, guided by what each school needs, i.e., job-a-likes,[8] school visits, visiting consultant workshops (shared cost) and conferences with staff facilitating.
EXTERNAL PROFESSIONAL LEARNING	Provided by an outside organization or specialist and provides an external certification, i.e., public registration workshops, conferences with professionals facilitating and visiting consultants.

---

7 This list was also created to demonstrate to staff that PD included more than just external workshops or visiting consultants, to encourage them to take greater ownership of their professional development, which they often complained was limited by budget.

8 These are often informal meetings between teachers from different schools, but who have the same or similar position, and share ideas or practices around a specific topic.

PERSONAL LEARNING NETWORK	Coordinated by the individual for their own needs, interests, and professional growth; likely to involve other professionals, i.e., professional reading, self-directed learning, social networks and online learning.

As highlighted in the following table, each strategy has a variety of positive and negative attributes that Renee and I have observed across hundreds of schools. These attributes are by no means a hard and fast rule and there are many exceptions, but they tend to be typical when there is no full-time PD Coordinator. Additionally, common areas of concern that schools need to consider for all four strategies are:

1. Participant learning needs aren't formerly assessed or surveyed in advance,
2. Staff aren't held accountable to any learning objectives, and
3. There are no tools to evaluate the application of learning. In the table, I also try to highlight some dependencies, as in what is required to ensure the PD is effective for that respective strategy.

PD Strategy	Positive	Negative	Dependencies
INTERNAL PROFESSIONAL LEARNING	• Inexpensive • Easy to schedule • Easy to differentiate • Focus on application	• Poor planning • Poor facilitation • No staff buy-in • Lack of expertise	• Facilitation • Planning time • Staff buy-in

NETWORK PROFESSIONAL LEARNING	• Inexpensive • Easy to differentiate • Gain outside perspective • Build school networks	• Difficult to schedule • Difficult to identify common needs	• Coordination with other schools • Clearly identified lead organizer(s)
EXTERNAL PROFESSIONAL LEARNING	• Good facilitation • Easy to coordinate • Build personal networks	• Expensive • Not contextualized for the teacher or their school • Difficult to assess the impact	• Training • Needs Assessment • Clear learning objectives
PERSONAL LEARNING NETWORK	• Inexpensive • Staff initiated • Easy to differentiate	• Doesn't encourage collaboration • Does not align with school objectives	• Include in the professional evaluation process

Leaders that are assigned the role of coordinating PD for middle leaders often have full-time teaching or administrative responsibilities, and in addition to a lack of time also have budgetary and resource constraints. For this reason, they are normally limited to one of the four strategies for professional learning, with internal professional learning being the most employed strategy.

An additional obstacle to coordinating effective PD is that PD Coordinators limit the scope of their role to specified periods of time, PD Days, which hinders staff from effectively applying professional learning. The obstacle to application is that the PD is occurring at a time when it is convenient for the school, not the educator.

PD days could be utilized more effectively if more time was allotted to plan productive sessions, which should include revisiting and bridging to past content as well as ensuring facilitators are well prepared. Unfortunately, though, Internal PD periods often devolve into unproductive discussions about work or are used to catch up on work. The greatest limitation of the most used form of PD is the inability to demonstrate good leadership, evidenced by thoughtful planning and strong facilitation skills.

What I propose and have been very successful in implementing with schools over the past 5 years, is a hybrid approach to utilizing all 4 strategies, aligned to practical learning objectives that I hold senior leaders accountable to understand and assess. Over the years I have learned, as an administrator and training provider, that whatever I can't do for lack of time or knowledge, I can outsource. This said, outsourcing comes at a high cost, so I can't outsource everything.

Many schools unfortunately take an all or nothing approach to developing their middle leaders, either by sending them to very expensive programs or not training them at all. The latter is justified by the belief they will learn on the job. The former fails to realize even though you pay a high cost to develop leadership capability, if you don't create an environment to apply what is learned, you are failing to develop the desired capacity. I know a lot of educators that understand the basic elements of good leadership but are incapable of demonstrating them. Which then begs the question, 'What did we get for all that money we invested?'

The hybrid option for developing middle leadership capacity requires every stakeholder involved in the process to be held accountable:

SENIOR LEADERS : Ensure buy-in, assess needs, provide networking opportunities, mentor middle leaders and assess impact of learning.

MIDDLE LEADERS : Demonstrate agency by seeking out additional resources to deepen understanding of relevant content, demonstrate the application, reflect and hone new skills.

FACILITATORS : Clearly communicate learning objectives, create interactive learning environments, understand participants' leadership goals and provide tools to assess the application.

The hybrid approach, when bolstered by all stakeholders being held accountable to the objective of capacity-building middle leaders to lead transformative collaboration, will prove to be the most effective.

A simple example of taking advantage of all four professional learning strategies might look like this:

INTERNAL PROFESSIONAL LEARNING	• Have cohorts meet to assess needs and identify training options; and • Invite in professional facilitators to ensure all middle leaders gain a broad perspective of multiple facets of effective leadership.
NETWORK PROFESSIONAL LEARNING	• Nominate or invite middle leaders to enroll for open registration leadership programs in groups of 2-4 per division and present key learnings to colleagues.
EXTERNAL PROFESSIONAL LEARNING	• Encourage middle leaders to host job-a-likes with peers in other schools to explore specific leadership topics.

PERSONAL LEARNING NETWORK	• Encourage middle leaders to document their leadership journey and publish it in relevant forums; • Supplement the purchase of leadership literature and online courses with the expectation that recipients of school funding will present key findings to colleagues; and • Encourage action learning projects bolstered by personal research.

70-20-10

A well-documented and thoroughly researched hybrid development strategy is the 70-20-10 rule of leadership development, where research has shown that 70% of leadership development comes from on-the-job work experience, and specifically overcoming challenges. 20% is support provided by superiors or coaches, and 10% is formal, structured learning. However, for on-the-job experience to be an effective form of professional development, senior leaders need to understand the requisite capacity that must be developed so that they can monitor and provide support as needed, which is largely what the 20% entails. Lastly, leadership development is not only a matter of being able to demonstrate the requisite skills, but also being able to develop those same skills in their team members.

An important consideration to understand to ensure the 70-20-10 rule is successful, is that of time. Proportionally, structured learning would appear to have a very small role, such as external workshops, conferences and diploma programs. However, they probably play the most significant role in the beginning, as this is where the seeds for development are planted and over time senior leaders need to tend to those seeds and cultivate them into a flourishing culture that will propel the school to realizing its core purpose. The 10% in the first year of capacity-building will actually be the bulk of the development activity, largely because middle leaders have full-time responsibilities to attend to and opportunities to apply lessons will be few and far between.

Opportunities to apply content will also need a large amount of support from senior leaders. It will take time for middle leaders to process all the new information. During this period senior leaders are reaffirming the learning objectives and helping middle leaders to understand the new content within their school context. At the beginning senior leaders also clearly have a larger role. Over time though, as middle leaders become more effective at seeking out learning opportunities, reflecting on what they are learning and honing their new knowledge and skills through application, the proportions take their proper shape.

Developing leadership capacity, in parallel with attending to regular work responsibilities, is a long process. In fact, it is a life-long process. The 70-20-10 rule for developing leadership capacity is the most effective process, but it takes a few years before these proportions can be sustained. This rule utilizes the positive attributes of all four professional learning strategies, emphasizes application and makes the role of all relevant stakeholders clear. There are obviously many components to each part of the rule to ensure it is not only effective, but also sustainable. Some of these I have mentioned throughout this chapter, such as:

1. Assessing learning needs;
2. Reflecting on how new knowledge can be applied in the current working environment;
3. Reflecting on the application of new knowledge; and
4. Honing this knowledge through repeated application.

These latter components, specifically that of reflection, is too easily overlooked. Learning is a continual process. In the beginning new or aspiring leaders rely on the facilitator to help them reflect on learning. This responsibility is then passed on to senior leaders. But if the aspiring leaders never take responsibility for this component, then their development can't be self-sustaining.

I believe that more can be learned from failure than from success, but only if we have the protocols and time to debrief the results. When we take time to diagnose and understand failure, we broaden our perspective to not only what didn't work, but also what other alternatives may exist to achieve the desired outcome. When we succeed, we often move on without taking time to understand if there were alternative paths to achieving the same outcome. Success with one unit, or over the course of one year, does not translate into success the next time that unit is taught or with a new class in the following year.

Innovation is a combination of recognizing a need and understanding that failure to address that need signifies the termination of one path to achieving the desired outcome. If success is to be replicated, we need to fully understand the environment required to achieve and sustain success, as well as what actions will lead to failure. The system reflects the team's ability to engage in processes that promote continuous improvement and the senior leader's understanding that teams need time to develop and execute those processes. When senior leaders capacity-build team leaders to achieve agreed-upon outcomes, and create the necessary environment for teams to succeed, the combined effect enables the school to achieve transformational outcomes.

SECTION 2

LEADING EFFECTIVE TEAMS

CHAPTER 7

TEAM FORMATION

Introduction

> "GETTING PEOPLE TO WORK TOGETHER ISN'T EASY, AND UNFORTUNATELY MANY LEADERS SKIP OVER THE BASICS OF TEAM BUILDING IN A RUSH TO START ACHIEVING GOALS. BUT YOUR ACTIONS IN THE FIRST FEW WEEKS AND MONTHS CAN HAVE A MAJOR IMPACT ON WHETHER YOUR TEAM ULTIMATELY DELIVERS RESULTS."
>
> – LEADING TEAMS: WHAT NEW TEAM LEADERS SHOULD DO FIRST, CAROLYN O'HARA, HARVARD BUSINESS REVIEW, SEPTEMBER 11, 2014

In the preceding chapters, I stated my case for how to:

1. Identify middle leaders based on the three dimensions of team, outcome, and capability, as well as the importance of why multiple stakeholders should be responsible for selecting middle leaders;
2. Recruit middle leaders to ensure cultural fit and why the expectations for each middle leader should be different;
3. Support middle leaders by breaking down silos and seeding a collaborative culture by establishing a middle leadership team;

4. Achieve transformative collaboration by giving middle leaders the mandate and support to pursue longer-term outcomes;
5. Empower middle leaders to innovate by building sandboxes; and
6. Build middle leadership capacity by investing time and money into their development, as well as allowing them to fail.

In the next five chapters, I outline sixteen hours of my foundational leadership program, "Leading Effective Teams." This program has evolved over ten years. Over 100 schools have participated in this program, either by contracting it as an in-service training or by regularly sending staff to my open registration events. The reason this program was developed was because at the time there was no leadership training for middle leaders that provided the operational and interpersonal skills necessary to lead teams effectively.

I am introducing this to you with the hope that you will be able to lead your middle leaders in a series of learning sessions that will help them better understand what you expect of them as leaders, as well as support them to lead transformative collaboration within their team.

Leading Effective Teams

Below is the introduction to the next five chapters, "Leading Effective Teams". If you plan on facilitating these next five chapters with one or more middle leaders, I suggest you introduce the learning engagement as follows:

ESSENTIAL QUESTION

What do middle leaders need to know and be able to do to pursue transformative outcomes and foster interdependency with their team?

OVERARCHING GOAL

By the end of the program (sixteen hours of facilitation), participants will understand how to facilitate team meetings (and have confidence to do so), manage difficult behaviors, mitigate conflict, and develop and foster strong relationships with and among team members.

WORKSHOP OUTCOMES
- *Participants explore the why, what, and how of transformative collaboration.*
- *Participants gain an understanding and appreciation of different leadership expectations.*
- *Participants practice effective communication skills.*
- *Participants gain an awareness of self and others and how to manage the disparity.*
- *Participants learn how to manage effective meetings, ensure equity, and foster interdependence.*
- *Participants learn how to enforce group norms and mitigate conflict within the team.*

METHODOLOGY

Survey plays an important role in shaping a learner's experience. To effectively facilitate this program participants are surveyed to understand their expectations, assess their familiarity with the proposed content, and identify possible case material for activities.

This program is broken into four 4-hour workshops. In each workshop, participants will be given reading assignments in advance to ensure a common understanding of the content to be facilitated, as well as assignments they will report on in the following workshop. The presenter facilitates each workshop, meaning learning will be activated and reinforced through discussion and team planning, not a lecture.

The rest of this chapter is devoted to how I frontload my "Leading Effective Teams" foundational program. The information below is either disseminated to participants in advance through relevant readings or introduced at the beginning of the first workshop.

Much of what has been discussed in previous chapters surfaces through discussions that occur throughout the program or in more specialized and advanced formats.

MICHAEL R. IANNINI

Getting Buy-In for the Program

This program has been contextualized for a multitude of audiences, such as Professional Learning Communities (PLCs), learning community leaders, teacher leaders, heads of department, accreditation teams, senior leadership teams, strategic task forces, and school boards. The readings selected are often related to the driving questions the participants have, which I discover through surveys and interviews, and support the topics for each workshop. In many cases, the content is new to even the most senior of leaders. For those who are familiar with the content and research, they are greatly satisfied by the ideas shared and consensus built through the activities that are facilitated.

Often, it is not so much what you want to introduce to your teams, but how it is facilitated that is important. This is because when the content is facilitated effectively, participants will be able to process and apply it to their context. This is more often achieved through experience sharing and generative exploration of a topic as opposed to what I refer to as spoon-feeding, which is when participants are given answers to problems and not pushed to resolve their own problems. Therefore, as you read and consider how to facilitate the activities I introduce, and most importantly, in the order that I introduce them, the critical key to success is seeding generative dialogue and ensuring that dialogue stays relevant to what you and your senior leaders believe the core purpose for the team is.

The content I introduce in this program and the activities supporting the content are derived from decades of research and documented organizational best practices across all industries and varying sizes of organizations. The activities that I am about to introduce have and will work for any type and level of team. These activities and tools can be found in any number of books or workshops. The activities from these various books or workshops effectively serve the same purpose, as they are all derived from the same studies conducted decades ago.

Lastly, it is essential for you to know my beliefs as they relate to being a facilitator. Although I have extensively studied leadership development and developed the leadership capacity of thousands of middle leaders, I never introduce myself as an expert; I am a facilitator.

HIDDEN IN PLAIN SIGHT

I always advise leaders to be facilitators of knowledge, not to present themselves as experts. Even if you have been a member of a successful Year-7 team in another school, it doesn't mean that success can be automatically replicated in Year-7 teams in other schools or even subsequent Year levels in the same school.

Experts are people who have a comprehensive and authoritative knowledge of or skill in a particular area. Experts are best positioned to transfer their knowledge and experience in the form of lectures and consulting. Facilitators, on the other hand, make an action or process easy or easier. Facilitators achieve this by properly assessing the capacity and capabilities of their audience, and then guide the audience to develop their capacity and capabilities to be experts in their own right. Experts often have a very deep and thorough understanding of specific processes, but will also require facilitation skills to ensure those processes can meet the needs of their audience.

Everything I teach is a culmination of my experiences, not only what I have done, but also what I have learned while working with thousands of educators. This is of course in addition to what I have researched to better understand the new challenges that schools face in an ever-changing world. In fact, most of my formative learning is the result of facilitating my middle leadership program.

These are my beliefs that have shaped the middle leadership program that I am sharing with you:

- You cannot be an effective curricular leader without understanding the operational levers of how an organization runs successfully, as well as possessing the interpersonal skills needed to coordinate the activities of people with disparate beliefs and value systems. Put another way, adding curricular to the word leader doesn't make it special; curricular is merely a descriptive term regarding the role of the leader.

- Schools are not unique organizations; they are organizations much like the largest bank or smallest restaurant. Organizations are formed to coordinate human activities to fulfil a vision. The success of the organization to fulfil that vision is a measure of the systems and processes it employs and its ability to manage those systems and processes effectively and efficiently.

- The ability to lead is not improved by what you study; it is improved by what you do and what you learn from what you did. Ideas for what and how we do something will derive from a need that can be influenced by books, workshops, and conversations with peers, but the ultimate development of leadership capacity is achieved by taking action.

- You don't need twenty years of experience or to be the head of a school to lead. David Brooks, an editorialist for the New York Times, stated it best in his February 8, 2018, op-ed, *Everyone a Changemaker*: "[Changemakers are] people who can see the patterns around them, identify the problems in any situation, figure out ways to solve the problem, organize fluid teams, lead collective action and then continually adapt as situations change."

- Don't use your boss or peers as an excuse to not lead. Managing up or across is only made more difficult by how you define your relationship with others. Effecting change in that relationship is leading, and it requires earning trust first and aligning goals second.

- You should always strive to do things better. Just because something may work now doesn't mean it will work tomorrow. Our world is constantly changing, and leaders need to help their organization adapt to those changes.

Lastly, I have one disclaimer I make to all participants in my leadership programs. For many people, these activities will not produce the desired result the first or even second time; however, each successive time they are facilitated, you will improve how you frontload the activity, set the environment for the activity, and facilitate the activity, ensuring the desired result is achieved. This latter point is not just a disclaimer but reinforces Belief-6, in that how you explain and get one team to understand an activity won't necessarily work with a different team. Each team will try to understand the activity and, more importantly, your motive for facilitating the activity, through the lens of their relationship with you and the stage of development the team is in. This latter concept is where the program begins.

Team Formation

The very first thing I ask Middle Leaders is, do they want to lead a Working Group or a Team? This answer will largely determine whether they should join the class, as I am capacity-building middle leaders to achieve transformational outcomes with a team.

I begin my engagement with middle leaders with a very simple activity. I introduce Google's Project Aristotle, and specifically how the authors of the project report define the difference between a Work Group and a Team:

Work groups *are characterized by the least amount of inter-dependence. They are based on organizational or managerial hierarchy. Work groups may meet periodically to hear and share information.*	**Teams** *are highly inter-dependent - they plan work, solve problems, make decisions, and review progress in service of a specific project. Team members need one another to get work done.*

If you only aspire to supervise a working group, there is no need to read further. Either I couldn't make the case for leading transformational collaboration, or it just isn't the right time for you to lead. For those that want to lead, let's start by assessing your team's capacity to engage in transformational collaboration.

One quick way to assess the capacity of a team is to understand its orientation to time. Time orientation is a cultural attribute; it's a cultural preference toward past, present, or future thinking. Time orientation affects how a culture values time and the extent to which it believes it can control time. Similarly, teams develop their own attitude toward time. Relating this cultural attribute to the collaboration spectrum, a transactional culture thinks in terms of how much time is left: i.e., "only 90 more days before the school year is over." On the other hand, a transformational culture thinks in terms of what they can achieve with the time they have. This latter frame of mind is incredibly powerful when teams are given a window of three years.

When working with team leaders, I can assess this attitude toward time by reviewing their team goals. Team leaders who see time as a hindrance to performance—for example, not having enough time—

will often focus on transactional goals. Team leaders who think in terms of what they can *achieve* in a given time will find time to achieve transformational goals. Thus, the most effective teams tend to recognize the time dilemma at the start of the school year, address it without being overwhelmed by the limitations, and therefore adapt to time constraints throughout the school year.

How do teams evolve to this level of effectiveness? One important attribute they exhibit is being future-oriented. Future-oriented teams delay immediate gratification by resisting the desire to pursue short-term, transactional goals. The issue of seeking immediate gratification is known as the urgency effect and was documented by Meng Zhu, Yang Yang, and Christopher K Hsee in a paper titled "The Mere Urgency Effect" in the *Journal of Consumer Research: "Normatively speaking,"* the researchers wrote, *"People may choose to perform urgent tasks with short completion windows, instead of important tasks with larger outcomes, because important tasks are more difficult and further away from goal completion, urgent tasks involve more immediate and certain payoffs, or people want to finish the urgent tasks first and then work on important tasks later."*

Immediate gratification in a school context is beginning the school year with unit planning, preparing the classroom, and attending to last-minute scheduling "emergencies." Because schools have been working from a calendaring template that is decades old, if not a century, staff return to school every year with a fixed mindset of what needs to be done and attend immediately to those tasks. These teams take for granted that they can tackle larger issues, such as transformational goals, once the school year is underway.

Unfortunately, setting out to achieve transformational work requires significant investments of time in building trust and aligning team member beliefs and interests. If this is not invested at the start of the school year, educators will fail to find time later. Thinking back to Chapter 5 and the case of Alexa, we can see how her ambitions were undermined largely because she didn't take time at the beginning of the school year to engage with and better understand the needs of everyone in her learning community. It wasn't until after that first disappointing meeting that she reflected on the relationships within the team and how they aligned with her ambitions.

Jeffrey T. Polzer (2003) found that the very first team meeting often becomes the norm for how teams operate. In the context of the team that gives in to immediate gratification, they reinforce informal norms for transactional collaboration and reinforce what Hargreaves and Dawe (1990) called *contrived collegiality*. The foundation for transformational collaboration requires alignment of beliefs and personal interests, as well as building consensus on behavioral norms that will enable constructive conflict. When teams do not begin the year by looking ahead, they allow a default set of norms to take shape. This default set of norms focuses on individual behaviors, as opposed to what Robert Garmston et al. introduced in their book *Adaptive Schools: Norms of Collaboration*.

Most team leaders will also fail to recognize their responsibility for team building and spend most of their time building relationships with individuals (Linda A. Hill, 1995). The combined effect of reinforcing transactional behaviors at the beginning of the school year and the team leader's focus on individual team performance will derail the potential for transformational collaboration. In fact, what I am describing here is not even a team; it is what Jeffrey T. Polzer (2003) calls a *manager-led working group*. It can be an effective way to manage specialist teams working to achieve predictable outputs, but it does not promote interdependence. It is unfortunately the level of cooperation that many leaders in school aspire to achieve in the span of a school year (Hollenbeck, *Journal of Applied Psychology*, 2002).

My work with schools also confirms this research, in that most teams I have observed struggle to conceive of any greater purpose than common planning and assessment. It is fair to say this is a reasonable goal for any new team leader in their first year. However, teams that have worked together for more than one year should be setting more ambitious goals: transformative goals. Transformative goals require vision, trust, and a future-oriented mindset.

A Year-6 team leader I coached had a vision to improve assessment practices across the elementary school. Unfortunately, she did not have the trust of senior leadership, because she was always critical of how they didn't have a coherent policy for assessment. The solution for the team leader was to engage with senior leadership in a series of informal meetings, each with only one main agenda item, to better understand their beliefs and envisioned future for assessment in the school. We then worked to model that envisioned future within her team, incorporating the team's own ideas and then documenting the results for her team. Senior leadership supported her to then share those results with other year-level leaders, which eventually led to senior leadership investing in several capacity-building initiatives and drafting a formal policy.

When reflecting on senior leadership's initial reticence to let the Year-6 team pursue their beliefs and ideas on assessment, I respect it due to the fear of what Michael Fullan termed as "innovation run amuck" in his article, *8 Forces for Leaders of Change*. Experienced leaders understand that even transactional activities can present unique challenges with a high potential for conflict. To successfully mitigate challenges and constructively leverage conflict, effective teams need to build trust and leverage each other's differences.

Without the trust and respect of one another, team members will be less likely to collaboratively problem-solve and more likely to walk away from conflict feeling wounded. Taking this into consideration, future-oriented teams will find time to build rapport with each other. Team members will understand how their values and beliefs are similar, as well as how they differ. Team leaders will align team members' values and identify behaviors that mitigate the disparate beliefs of the team. These teams understand that teams develop in stages, so they begin the school year by doing the following:

- Working to develop trust and understanding how each other is different,
- Agreeing on a list of appropriate team values and the behaviors that demonstrate those values, and
- Building consensus on a team mission that will guide the work of the team.

Let's begin by understanding how teams develop, discussing the middle leader's role in building an effective team, and introducing the activities that facilitate the development of the team. Tuckman's model for staged team development is probably the most referenced: **Forming, Storming, Norming, Performing, and Adjourning.**

HIDDEN IN PLAIN SIGHT

Below is an abridged excerpt from *Leading Effective Meetings, Teams, and Work Groups in Districts and Schools* by Matthew Jennings, which is the best summary of Tuckman's Stages contextualized for schools. The periods of time noted in parentheses refer to the amount of time Jennings believed these stages required for task forces and committees to move through each stage:

FORMING (2-3 MONTHS)	During this phase, group members still don't know much about the other members or the group process; as a result, communication tends to be tentative and characterized by a lot of agreement, as any conflict tends to be downplayed or ignored. Primary concerns at this stage include getting to know one another, becoming oriented to the group's goals, establishing operating procedures, and obtaining task-relevant information...
STORMING (1-2 MONTHS)	Once the "honeymoon period" of the forming stage is over, members begin to vie for control of the group. Members can become emotional or resistant at this stage, and the mood can turn hostile as disagreements are expressed. Even when the discussion remains focused on the task, individuals tend to take sides, form coalitions, and align themselves with different factions; members must attempt to develop processes for resolving their differences. This phase is the most complex, yet it is critical to success because it allows the group to air and clarify significant issues. Members must strive for consensus and try to prevent winners and losers...

NORMING (1-2 MONTHS)	As the Storming Stage subsides, group members begin to sense that a positive development is occurring; though interactions remain tentative, members tend to express their opinions and cooperate more. The group becomes less polarized and more cohesive as disagreements turn toward possible solutions...
PERFORMING (4-7 MONTHS)	At this stage, group members share their viewpoints and information, seeking to achieve consensus on the final decisions and follow through on them. Members feel a sense of relief as tension is replaced by group cohesion and problem-solving predominates...

Doing some simple math, it is easy to see that, at a minimum, going through all four stages would take a complete school year, and this doesn't include the last and most important stage, "Adjourning." It is during this stage that experiences and lessons during the preceding stages are codified into knowledge that the team, and its respective members, can reference and build upon future projects.

Adjourning also communicates that Tuckman's Stages have a beginning and an ending. These are stages teams move through relative to some outcome they seek to achieve. When that outcome is achieved, they debrief it and move on. When they move on and identify a new outcome to achieve, they will move back through these stages. The duration of each stage varies based on the team members' ability to negotiate and overcome the challenges that define each stage.

Obviously, a team that has a long history of achieving outcomes together will move faster through the stages than a team that has constant turnover. But, related to my Belief-6, just because a team was able to successfully work together to achieve one outcome does not mean they will be able to work successfully to achieve another outcome. Even the most well-established teams need to always start in the Forming Stage when confronting a new challenge or pursuing a new goal. And, in many cases, some teams may never get to the

Adjourning stage, let alone the Performing Stage, if they are unable to resolve conflict.

It is also important to note that these stages are not fixed. For example, future-oriented teams understand that even though some planning activities cannot be delayed, they still need to make time for team building each year. Teams that are aware of these stages can progress quickly through them by doing some activities simultaneously, but if they find themselves stuck, they will have to return to the beginning to reaffirm roles and processes based on what they have learned. It is not uncommon for a team to learn how to mitigate conflict and have a sense of group efficacy but not achieve the results they hoped for. It is for this reason that teams need to regularly debrief their performance to ensure they are on track. If an output is not produced, or fails to meet expectations, then the team should re-examine the output's relationship to the outcome and question if there are other antecedents that precede that output.

My last piece of advice about team formation, and the order in which activities should take place, is that goal setting should be the final activity in the Forming Stage. In terms of a normal school year, team goals should be discussed one to two months into the school year. The rationale for this is because it takes time to establish the sandbox in which you will pursue the desired outcome. The Forming Stage is the period in which you confirm how much capacity the team has, understand the needs and wants of those who will be playing in the sandbox, and identify competing external initiatives that will erode the current capacity.

CHAPTER 8

WORKSHOP 1

Building Trust

Let's begin by building trust and taking time to understand how each team member views the world through the lens of their own value and belief systems. Once we are able to identify the values and beliefs each team member holds, we will be able to draft a team statement of purpose that makes explicit why the team exists, how they will work together, and what they seek to achieve.

The activities in this and the next chapter can be facilitated in less than three hours and should be done in the team's very first meeting. The time varies depending on how much time the team spends debriefing each activity. Preparation can take three to six hours because as a facilitator you need to rehearse how to introduce the activity, or what I refer to as frontloading, as well as be prepared for a variety of outputs, some of which may not be desired. This preparation is necessary, and provides an example of why middle leaders need additional time and resources to effectively execute their responsibilities.

First, let's understand why we begin with surfacing values. Our behaviors reflect our beliefs, and our belief systems are influenced by our values. Therefore, to ensure team members are intrinsically motivated, and that they appreciate the lens through which their peers view the world, we need to identify and define all the values that will influence the work of the team. Furthermore, to mitigate conflict and harness it as a tool to innovate, we need to appreciate how our peers may perceive the environment differently.

This is easier said than done, as values are very difficult to define, and our answers can be influenced by the context in which we are asked. Therefore, we need to devise a strategy for surfacing values specific to the context of the team. Our values reflect how we feel the world should operate, and when we observe something (news article, movie, student observation) that mirrors those values, it will arouse us emotionally. To surface a person's values, we need to evoke an emotional response that inspires them.

Three-Quote Draw

The activity I feel is the best way to surface individual team member values is a card game a consultant from the National School Reform Foundation introduced to me when he assisted me in co-facilitating a program related to Professional Learning Communities. I have adapted this activity to ensure that its output contributes to the desired outcome for the end of this workshop. This first activity is also a great opportunity for me to explain how activities should be designed and facilitated.

In any activity we introduce, we need to answer the quintessential question of "why." Why are we doing this? When we break from routine and ask our peers to engage in an activity they feel doesn't directly contribute to their work, they will want to know why. The introduction in the previous chapter, as well as the preceding paragraphs, should be enough to answer the question of "why" for this activity: to surface personal values related to teaching and learning.

In my experience as a facilitator, I have found that famous quotes appear to be the fastest and easiest way to elicit a compelling emotional response or inspiration. Therefore, to surface individual team member's values, we want them to choose a quote that personally inspires them. In order to motivate us to achieve transformational outcomes, we need our work to also inspire us. We need to connect what we do with who we are. For others to truly understand the emotional response, we need to capture it in the moment that it occurs. Team-building activities require team members to engage in a shared experience and experience each other's emotional responses at that moment.

This activity requires forty to fifty quotes that can come from a range of sources and cultures, including but not limited to sports, business, religion, literature, media, politics, education, and philosophy.

A shortcut to collecting all these quotes would be to ask teachers, not on your team, in various subjects or grade levels, for four to five quotes they find inspirational. This is also a great way to accrue quotes if you need to facilitate this activity for people from different languages and cultural backgrounds.

In regard to using quotes originating from a different language or culture, I have had several quotes translated from English to Mandarin Chinese and found my audiences to be equally receptive to the activity. However, be mindful if quotes have sub-context, such as Chinese idioms, several of which require anecdotal context to understand. It is also important to identify the origin of the quote, as sometimes it is not so much what is said, but who said it, that can excite someone. Ultimately, we are trying to trigger an emotional response, and to accomplish this we need to cast as large a net as possible without making the activity too burdensome.

The main objective of a facilitator is to expose team members to as many quotes as possible in as short of time as possible. As the facilitator, you have already been exposed to all the quotes and probably have even chosen your favorite. Make a copy of that quote and put it aside so that you can share it at the end of the activity. As the facilitator, you are the dealer and have the ultimate responsibility to keep the activity moving. By keeping the activity moving fast, you can prevent analysis paralysis, where people spend too long trying to decipher the meaning of a quote, which will limit the number of quotes a person reads, as well as dilute any potential emotional response. The main objective as a participant is to choose the quote that elicited the strongest emotional response upon initially reading the quote. If the quote didn't trigger a response, then swiftly move on to the next quote.

The following activity will take thirty minutes to facilitate for a team of four to eight people. With this approach, a team can identify and define values that will contribute to the drafting of their team statement of purpose. This activity can be adapted for much larger groups, which makes a great icebreaker for an entire faculty to participate in. My suggestion for larger groups, such as the whole faculty, is limiting table groups to eight people while ensuring each group is using the same set of cards.

Preparation for this activity will require chart paper, felt tip markers, and a minimum of forty inspirational quotes printed on cardstock cut to the size of playing cards. If you can laminate the cards, it makes playing easier and the cards will last longer. This game emulates a card game, so create an environment befitting a card game, such as a round table with nothing on the surface that will obstruct the dealing of cards. The rules are simple:

STEP 1	Deal three cards to each participant.
STEP 2	Give each participant one-minute to read the cards they have been dealt and select one card they like the most. This may cause some stress at first, so don't be too strict enforcing the time limit, but do make people mindful of the time.
STEP 3	The other two cards are passed to the left and the dealer discards their two cards by putting them at the bottom of the deck and gives the person on their left two new cards.
STEP 4	Give participants one minute to review and select one card they want to keep and then pass two cards they don't want to the left.
STEP 5	Continue for 8 to 10 rounds with each person keeping only one card at the end of each round.
STEP 6	For the last round, after participants have selected the one card they wish to keep, have them pass the two cards directly back to the dealer.

STEP 7	At this point, this activity can serve two purposes, one of which is what I have intended for the purpose of this book, to surface values and actions that will become the core of the work the team does. Another purpose is for a full faculty team building.
	
	For Faculty Team Building:
	
	1. Once everyone has selected a card, ask everyone to stand up and separately seek out 3 staff members that were sitting at different tables and share their quotes and why they chose it.
	2. Ask everyone to sit down after they introduced their quote 3 times, and heard 3 different people introduce their quotes.
	3. Debrief and close out the activity with these questions:
	   • What did you think of this process?
	   • What have you learned about your colleagues?
	   • Did anyone find another person with the same quote, or get introduced to a quote they wish they had chosen? If yes, what did that feel like?
	   • How can we use this knowledge of our colleagues to drive collaboration?
	
	For the purposes of surfacing values that inspire team members and actions they will be compelled to take; write at the top of a piece of chart paper or whiteboard, visible to everyone, these three questions:
	
	1. What quote did you choose and why?
	2. What does this quote compel you to want to do?
	3. What personal values (maximum of three) do you think best represents why you chose that quote?

STEP 8	Give participants one minute to quietly consider their answers to those questions. Ensure no one is talking during this time.
STEP 9	Create two columns on the chart paper, and at the top of one write "Do" and at the top of the other write "Values." Now ask for a volunteer to share their answers.
STEP 10	Give each person two to three minutes to speak; at the end of that time, summarize in the first column, in as few of words as possible, actions the quote inspires to be taken, and in the other column the values that the quote represents.
STEP 11	Once every team member has shared, build consensus on three actions and three values the team wants to have at the center of their work. These will be synthesized into the team's statement of purpose.

The values and actions surfaced in this activity become very important team planning tools, not only for developing a Statement of Purpose for the team, which will be discussed in Chapter 9, but for meeting management, mitigating conflict and assessing team health. In terms of these latter three leadership responsibilities, as a team leader, we need to make sure we make time to talk about things that matter to our team, identify and support actions that the team believes in, and reflect on how those discussions and actions have contributed to the team, school and most importantly, student learning.

Implicit Leadership Theory

Next, we need to clarify the role of the leader and understand the expectations that team members have for the team leader. The following activity also serves another purpose: to identify leadership behaviors that will motivate and inspire the team, and that all team members will be expected to demonstrate. To achieve this, I often use a forming activity based on **Implicit Leadership Theory (ILT).**

ILT states that individual beliefs about personal attributes (personality, skills, and behaviors) contribute to or impede outstanding leadership (Javidan et al., 2006). Some examples of personal attributes that team members might find favorable in a leader would be *trustworthy, visionary, risk-taking,* and *decisive.* The importance of surfacing these beliefs is that we will build awareness of each other's expectations for how the team will be led, as well as develop a greater understanding of team members' expectations for how they should behave when assuming accountability for the team. Please note that in this activity you will be surfacing beliefs; beliefs are influenced by values, and you will want to connect the outputs of this activity to the first activity.

ILT is drawn from extensive research into cross-cultural leadership, specifically, data collected from the Globe Study *(https://globe. bus.sfu.ca/).* Based on this research, we know that some leadership characteristics are universally desired, whereas some may only be desired in specific cultures. *Trustworthy* and *visionary* are examples of universally desired leadership characteristics, whereas *risk-taking* and *decisive* are desirable to only certain cultures. By surfacing these beliefs early, team members gain a greater appreciation for how they as team members are similar, and, more important, how they differ in terms of how they want the team managed. They can use this awareness to begin developing communication and working strategies early in the school year. When confronted with challenges or conflict, team members will be more likely to address the problem and not make inferences about team member behaviors.

Similar to the last activity, the output for this activity will be to build consensus on three leadership characteristics that the team agrees will motivate and inspire them. These three leadership characteristics will be synthesized into the group norms activity that will be introduced next, as well as the team statement of purpose. This activity is appropriate for any team size and can be adapted for larger groups that are looking to explore cross-cultural leadership dynamics.

This activity will take approximately thirty minutes and requires pens, note-taking paper, chart paper, and felt tip markers.

1. The facilitator will first introduce ILT and its application for understanding cross-cultural leadership dynamics.

2. Each team member will be asked to silently envision a leader that they have found to be influential in their life, either someone they have worked with, a celebrity, a family member, or anyone else whose leadership has inspired them. Make sure all participants are quiet during this reflection, which should take no longer than three minutes.

3. After about a minute, some participants will be ready to proceed, so tell the group to remain silent and to think of the leadership characteristics that contribute to this person being a great leader, and then list a minimum of five of those characteristics.

4. Once everyone has listed at least five characteristics, ask someone to be the note taker, whose job will be to list all the characteristics that are identified.

5. Ask each participant to share one item from his or her list and not to repeat an item mentioned by someone else. Some characteristics will be similar in meaning but may be referred to differently, such as *visionary* and *big picture person*; try to group these together.

6. After everyone has shared their list and the note taker has compiled all responses, the group should vote on the top three leadership characteristics that the team leader, and more importantly, all team members, should demonstrate in their working environment.

The Elephant in the Room

The next forming activity that needs to be facilitated is building consensus on group norms. I love facilitating this activity, as it is a form of therapy. It allows team members to reflect on all the things that disappointed or angered them about past teamwork and surface it in a productive and positive way. I call this activity *the Elephant in the Room*. This is an American expression that means: a major problem or controversial issue that is obviously present but avoided as a subject for discussion because it is more comfortable to do so. Examples of *elephants* in your team meeting room would be when some team members use their phone or laptops in meetings, which undermines trust because we assume those people don't care about what is being said, BUT, no one wants to address it, because *'we are all professionals'* so why should we even have to tell them that.

Similar to the ILT activity, we will need a facilitator, note taker, pens, note-taking paper, chart paper, and felt tip markers. The instructions are as follows:

1. Draw participants' attention to the list of values and leadership characteristics that were previously agreed on.

2. Ask participants to write a list of ten things they hate about working in teams when those values and/or leadership characteristics are not present, i.e., not understanding the purpose of the work, inappropriate communication, social loafers, negativity, etc. During this time there is no talking, but expect giggling. Give everyone two to three minutes to complete his or her list. Don't be afraid to use the word *hate*, either. We want to surface the most frustrating issues of working in a team— or, in other words, the *elephants*.

3. Have each person in turn read one item from their list and continue having team members read one item from their lists until all items have been presented. Allow people to share anecdotes of why they included an item in their list. The anecdotes are, in essence, the *group therapy*, but limit sharing to one minute.

4. Do not let people read their whole list at once, as there will be overlaps that will prevent others from fully participating.

5. Remind people to present the item they share in terms of how it impacts team performance, and, most important, do not include names. This latter requirement, when mentioned in step two, always gets laughter, adding to the positive vibe of this activity.

6. After the consolidated list of items is complete, build consensus on five behaviors all team members agree will impede the performance of the team.

7. Do not try to agree on more than five. The time and attention of the team are limited. You want them focused on collaborating, not policing each other. Hence it is crucial to focus on behaviors that will drive collaboration.

8. Delve deeper into each negative behavior, such as inappropriate communication, to understand and agree on specific behaviors that we agree need to be stopped. For example, is it team members dominating discussions or being overly negative about others' ideas?

9. Push the group to be as specific as possible about the behaviors that will impede team performance. If the behavior we target is too ambiguous, then conflict will arise when we try to hold team members accountable to the norms. The conflict will be born of how the norm is interpreted; therefore, be as specific as possible.

10. Reframe the negative behaviors into desired behaviors. For example, if social loafing is a behavior we want to mitigate, then the desired behavior could be, "Come to all meetings prepared to contribute."

11. Compare the list of five positive behaviors to the actions inspired by the quotes identified in the first activity. Try to find ways to synthesize the actions and the five positive behaviors. Team members will be more mindful of behaviors that are representative of their core values.

12. Lastly, once all negative behaviors are reframed, rewrite them on a clean piece of chart paper so that they can be displayed in all team meetings. These can also be listed on all team agendas.

Group Norms

I have some important notes about group norms, or, as some schools might refer to them, social contracts or essential agreements. First, the purpose of the team is to work together to achieve some purpose. For organizations to work, they need systems to run efficiently and stakeholder alignment to operate effectively. Group norms are not only a type of system to hold team members accountable for behaviors that impede performance, but they also align team members' values, beliefs, and behaviors. However, the purpose of this system is not to modify behaviors, which is why we don't frame the norm as being negative. You do not want the time and attention of the team focusing on policing behaviors.

Here is one last note about the types of behaviors we want to focus on: Similar to how we have transactional and transformative forms of collaboration, there are transactional and transformative behaviors that teams should encourage. A few examples of transactional behaviors that are vital to a team, are: complete tasks in a timely manner, show up to meetings on time, be prepared and pay attention in meetings. Coming late to meetings, not reading the agenda, and sending emails in meetings are examples of the things people hate in meetings, yet these behaviors are seldom addressed. Therefore, team leaders at first may need to address these issues before the team can evolve to a more transformative state.

Norms are not fixed. They need to change as the team develops. Each of Tuckman's Stages effectively requires different norms to move through that stage. As the team evolves, it will confront new challenges, thus necessitating focusing on new norms. Robert Garmston et al., in their book, *Adaptive Schools*, recommend that as a team evolves to a more collaborative state, they need to be aware of and capacity build the capability of demonstrating these seven norms:

1. PAUSING
   Pausing before responding or asking a question allows time for thinking and enhances dialogue, discussion, and decision-making.

2. PARAPHRASING
   Using a paraphrase starter that is comfortable for you – "So..." or "As you are..." or "You're thinking..." – and following the starter with an efficient paraphrase assists members of the group in hearing and understanding one another as they converse and make decisions.

3. POSING QUESTIONS
   Two intentions of posing questions are to explore and to specify thinking. Questions may be posed to explore perceptions, assumptions, and interpretations, and to invite others to inquire into their thinking. For example, "What might be some conjectures you are exploring?" Use focusing

questions such as, "Which students, specifically?" or "What might be an example of that?" to increase the clarity and precision of group members' thinking. Inquire into others' ideas before advocating one's own.

4. PUTTING IDEAS ON THE TABLE
   Ideas are the heart of meaningful dialogue and discussion. Label the intention of your comments. For example: "Here is one idea..." or "One thought I have is..." or "Here is a possible approach..." or "Another consideration might be..."

5. PROVIDING DATA
   Providing data, both qualitative and quantitative, in a variety of forms supports group members in constructing shared understanding from their work. Data have no meaning beyond that which we make of them; shared meaning develops from collaboratively exploring, analyzing, and interpreting data.

6. PAYING ATTENTION TO SELF AND OTHERS
   Meaningful dialogue and discussion are facilitated when each group member is conscious of self and of others, and is aware of what (s)he is saying and how it is said as well as how others are responding. This includes paying attention to learning styles when planning, facilitating, and participating in group meetings and conversations.

7. PRESUMING POSITIVE INTENTIONS
   Assuming that others' intentions are positive promotes and facilitates meaningful dialogue and discussion, as well as prevents unintentional put-downs. Using positive intentions in speech is one manifestation of this norm.

I wholeheartedly agree with these norms for collaboration. Demonstrating these behaviors will promote transformative collaboration. I feel the Seven Norms of Collaboration are the best examples of the types of norms teams should be holding each other accountable, in order to work effectively in a transformative state. Additionally, I recommend that a team should only focus on one norm at a time. A team should evaluate the team's effectiveness to demonstrate that norm after every meeting. Once the team has developed expertise in demonstrating behaviors related to that norm they can begin focusing on the next norm. This said, you can only begin focusing on norms at this level of awareness provided the transactional norms, such as not sending emails in meetings and arriving unprepared, have been dealt with, otherwise they can easily undermine the Seven Norms of Collaboration.

Once the norms for working in a transformative state are established, the team leader must consistently reinforce them with the intention of empowering team members to take ownership of the norms. A team's ability to move from the Forming Stage to the Norming Stage, which can happen within six months, will be whether team members actively enforce the norms without the need of the team leader having to police individual team member behavior. In between these stages is the Storming Stage. During that period, team leader will need to be focused on team member behaviors and demonstrate how to draw awareness to those behaviors without creating conflict.

CHAPTER 9
ESTABLISHING PURPOSE

> "IDENTITY REPRESENTS THE STORY THAT A GROUP TELLS ITSELF TO ORGANIZE ITS VALUES AND BELIEFS. A GROUP'S BELIEFS DETERMINE ITS BEHAVIOR. COLLECTIVELY, ITS BEHAVIOR AFFECTS STUDENT LEARNING."
>
> – ROBERT DILTS [9]

Three important outputs have been yielded from the Forming activities in the last chapter. These are:

1. An agreed-upon set of values that are essential to inspire team members to achieve transformative outcomes;
2. An agreed-upon set of beliefs about leadership and compelling actions the team should take, aligned with the team's values; and
3. An agreed-upon set of behaviors that the team will demonstrate in their work together.

These outputs are essential for establishing a team's core purpose, the reason why they exist.

---

9 Dilts, R. (1994). *Effective presentation skills*. Capitola, CA: Meta.

Guiding Statements Explained

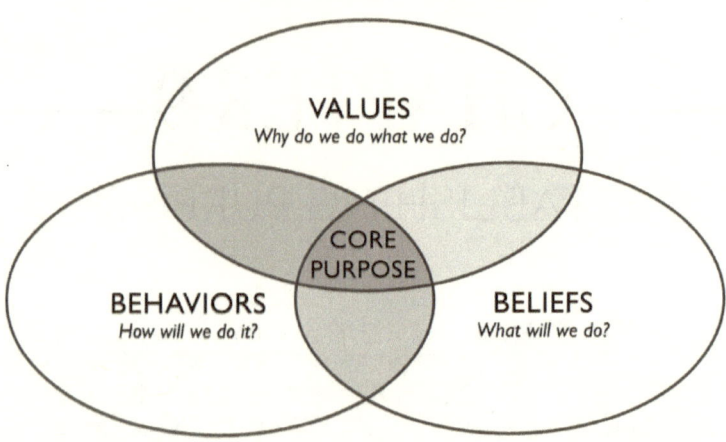

The best way to explain *Core Purpose*, featured in this image, is to understand this quote from Jim Collins, the father of the concept of going from *Good to Great*:

> "COMPANIES THAT ENJOY ENDURING SUCCESS HAVE CORE VALUES AND A CORE PURPOSE THAT REMAINS FIXED WHILE THEIR BUSINESS STRATEGIES AND PRACTICES ENDLESSLY ADAPT TO A CHANGING WORLD... A PRIMARY ROLE OF CORE PURPOSE IS TO GUIDE AND INSPIRE."
> – JAMES C. COLLINS AND JERRY I. PORRAS [10]

Jim Collins' research and writing related to company sustainability and growth has not only popularized this field of management consulting, but also has demystified the process of aligning strategy

---

[10] James C. Collins and Jerry I. Porras, *Building Your Company's Vision*, Harvard Business Review, September–October 1996.

with vision, and team goals with strategy. A quick summary of his ideas would be that vision, or what schools refer to as their guiding statements, is made up of three components:

1. Timeless unchanging core values;
2. Fundamental reason for existence, beyond making money, often referred to as its mission or core purpose; and
3. Huge and audacious, yet achievable, aspirations for the future.

Of these three components, core values are the most important to great, enduring organizations. The reason for this, is we can't change our values, and any attempt to do so would be superficial at best. Many teams suffer from this dilemma of superficiality; they are pursuing objectives that they don't believe in, and feel aren't representative of the school's vision. The result of not having our values at the core of our work is that inferior products will be produced. Michael Fullan refers to this as "moral purpose."

An organization's mission needs to also be enduring because it makes explicit the organization's fundamental reason for existence. Realizing an organization's fundamental reason for existence is an ongoing process that requires constant alignment. Finally, Collins states that great organizations need *BHAGs—Big Hairy Audacious Goals*—or what many organizations would refer to as the strategy. The strategy does change over time as we grow and is confronted with new challenges. In the face of adversity, we don't change who we are; we change how we address it. The image below is a representation of what organizational alignment looks like.

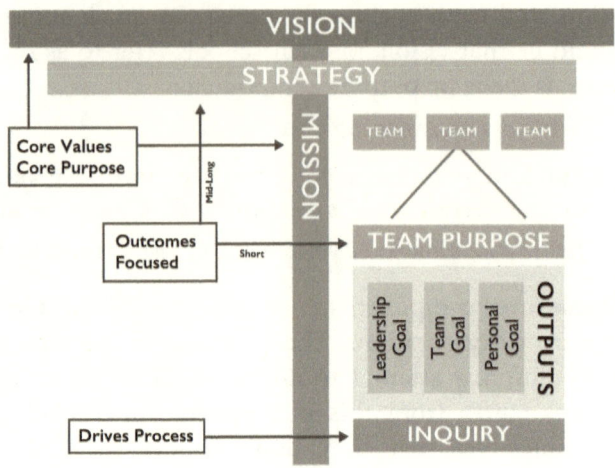

An organization's *vision* addresses the question of "why" and tells a compelling story of what it will look like when that vision is actualized. An organization's *mission* is like a load-bearing support; it provides guidance to management on how it should develop strategies to realize the vision. A school's strategy is meant to be responsive to the short- and long-term operating environments, market conditions, and changing demographics that the school must respond to realize its vision. Teams are tasked with implementing the strategy; therefore, a *team purpose* needs to align with the strategy.

If the strategy is reactive, not proactive, it most likely won't take into consideration the core values and core purpose of the school. An example of being reactive is when school leadership create initiatives in response to parent feedback or emerging pedagogical trends, without evaluating these initiatives and trends against its existing guiding statements. Often this type of strategy is translated into several transactional tasks that teams must complete. When this happens, there is very little buy-in, and middle leaders won't be able to align individual team members with the strategy. In the end, it is just more work for staff, which may get completed, but it won't be *great*.

Many schools I work strategically with are concerned about enrolment. In many cases, I push them further, asking why enrolment is at the center of their attention. Usually, it takes a few whys to get to the heart of the issue, but what is often the concern is that if there aren't enough students in grade level, or perhaps in secondary school, where many independent schools tend to have lower enrolment, then they can't offer certain programs deemed critical to realizing its mission.

An example of this would be a school that wants to prepare students to be global citizens but has to limit its humanity classes due to low enrolment. Unfortunately, for many schools, the focus of enrolment is not values-driven. Even worse, enrolment-related strategies are often driven by perceived community needs that end up translating into staff doing tasks that conflict with their own values and beliefs. For example, schools that try to increase enrolment by being more inclusive without setting the foundation to support prospective students will disrupt both the teaching and learning environments for students and teachers.

Even though schools operate on a much smaller scale than the types of companies Collins researched and wrote about, the fundamental organizational structure and governance of schools is not so different. Schools, like Fortune 100 companies, can be dramatically impacted by social and political forces, thus causing an organization's values to be periodically tested and its mission constantly questioned. In the face of adversity, a school shouldn't deviate from its core values to appease social and political pressures. Nor should it rearticulate or redefine its mission to appease changing demographics.

In Collins' research, he found it was better for an organization to stay true to its values and serve another market than give in to the pressures from the current market. The reason for this is simple: if we can't defend our basic values and engage in meaningful work, the work we do won't be great. Therefore, teams must establish their purpose relative to the school's strategy in their own statement of purpose. All manner of conflict can be mitigated and harnessed for the good of the students if team members' values are aligned and clearly present in the work that they do.

Goal Setting

At the end of the Forming Stage, we will know the team's capacity and capabilities to pursue goals that support the team's statement of purpose. The three types of goals every team should have are: 1) a team goal, 2) personal goals, and 3) a leadership goal.

A team goal is something no one team member can achieve on their own. It is the most significant output that contributes to the team's statement of purpose. Team member's personal goals are intended to connect an individual's interests and professional inquiries with the work of the team. Fulfilling the personal goal should be an output that contributes to the team goal. A leadership goal is more than just a personal goal for the team leader. It addresses the prospective challenges the team will face to work interdependently toward its purpose.

Let's use the previous grade-level team statement of purpose as an example: *To develop the dispositions and skills in Grade 6 students that will support more effective agents of learning.* First, our desired outcome is for students to take greater ownership in their learning. Keeping in mind Jennifer Nahrgang's observations, the team goal needs to be inclusive of all team members and should be written to explicitly state how the team will achieve the goal. Here is an example: *We will use 20% of our common planning time to learn how to observe and provide feedback to one another to inform teaching practices as they relate to the team mission.*

The difference between a team statement of purpose and a goal is that a statement of purpose is *outcomes-focused*, encouraging students to take more ownership of their learning. Goals are *output*-focused; a significant goal, in this case, is capacity-building the team to be able to observe instances of agency (students taking ownership of learning) and being able to report that to team members in a constructive manner.

As for personal goals, these could relate to the various instances of agency that team members will observe; for example: *I will ensure that once per week, students devise and pursue one relevant inquiry into unit content.* Other team members may want to work with subject specialist teachers to understand how they can integrate music, arts, or even physical education into their lesson planning, provided the goal is written in such a way that it supports agency.

Taking into account that a team purpose will require a high degree of interdependency, particularly in giving and receiving feedback, an appropriate leadership goal would be: *I will study various strategies and tools to evaluate team performance so that I can objectively inform the team once per month about how we are performing relative to our goal, and be able to constructively give feedback to individual team members regarding their goals.*

These goals are fairly **SMART (Specific – Measurable – Attainable – Relevant – Time-Bound);** however, to achieve these goals, there are several activities that must take place. Where does one begin with their goal? The answer is actually a question. By definition, a goal is a desired result; it is not a plan, it is merely a target. You still need to figure out how to achieve it.

A *professional inquiry* focuses on structures and processes. The concept of a professional inquiry is unique to education, but the idea that an investigation should begin with a question is common across all industries and professions. During my break from education, I studied and also had several responsibilities related to project management. To be an effective project manager, you had to be able to introduce a compelling business argument for what you were tasked to achieve, as well as explain the problem being addressed. The problem was drafted as a question: *How will we identify and document instances of agency so we can establish a benchmark to evaluate student agency against?*

For a project manager, goals are milestones or targets that inform all stakeholders of their progress toward answering that question. However, to answer the question, several other questions needed to be surfaced, documented, and answered. For example:

- How do we define agency?
- What are age-appropriate instances of agency?
- What do we want to document?

It is not enough to simply ask the questions; they need to be recorded, as they are part of the road map. The answer to each question is a mini goal—an output that contributes to the greater output and ultimately the outcome. It is for this reason that inquiry drives goals, which contribute to the team's purpose.

One final point before we move on. SMART goals are not good for teams, as Jennifer Nahrgang indicated when referring to learning goals. Although it is a useful acronym, many leaders—and schools for that matter—begin and end their goal setting with writing SMART goals. They neglect to support those goals with a compelling case for why it is important, or clearly explain how the problem it will solve. Furthermore, SMART goals are statements that tell people what they *need* to do; they don't tell them *how*. If the process and end point are straightforward, then I would argue it is not a goal, but merely a task. Goals are meant to develop us; they shouldn't be confused as having more work. The reward should be some measurable increase in confidence, knowledge, or skills, rather than some transactional goal, such as completing lesson plans or planning a student's performance.

Drafting a Statement of Purpose

This last Forming activity is crucial for highly effective teams to engage in but is usually taken for granted. Most schools have their own statement of core purpose, or mission, and senior leaders regularly argue with me that they don't want teams or personnel drafting their own. The reason for this is twofold: First, they fear that teams will act in self-interest and choose a purpose that does not serve the greater good. Second, their experience with drafting guiding statements is at the organizational level, which are complex and time-consuming, therefore they do not want their teams rearticulating statements that many senior leaders feel are self-explanatory.

Highly successful organizations, though, encourage developing and aligning mission statements (statements of purpose) throughout the organization: at the organization level, team level, and personal level. Obviously, at each higher level in the organization, the process is much more complex and time-consuming, but this is also why at each higher level, those mission statements need to be more enduring. A personal mission statement should be done yearly, a team's mission statement should last two to five years, and an organizational mission statement should last ten to thirty years. We need to always be reminded of "why we do what we do." The mission statement, or what I introduce in this chapter as a team's statement of purpose, is a powerful facilitation tool to ensure effective meeting management and mitigate conflict.

Below is an example of how to align mission and goals across the school. For this example, I am going to use the guiding statements of a school, in which I did governance and leadership consulting from 2014-2016, the American International School of Guangzhou.

I find these statements compelling and crafted correctly, in a way that the vision identifies the core values, and the mission defines the core purpose [11]:

SCHOOL VISION	A leader of dynamic, compassionate, and connected learning.
SCHOOL MISSION	To nurture future-ready individuals to aspire, achieve, and contribute.
BOARD MISSION	To ensure the long-term viability and be good stewards of the school's resources, we will think individually and act collectively to focus on the big picture, manage boundaries, and monitor performance.
LEADERSHIP MISSION	To empower our colleagues to innovate, engage with our community to ensure the needs of all learners are met and to continually evaluate our programs to ensure they are preparing our students for tomorrow.
GRADE-LEVEL MISSION	To develop the dispositions and skills in Grade 6 students that will support more effective agents of learning.

A much easier way to demonstrate the importance of this process is to ask staff to explain what their job is and why they do it. Then ask them to read the organization's mission statement. Next, ask them to explain how their job supports that mission. Their answer is effectively a personalized version of the organization's mission statement, reworded to suit their context. What they craft will feel empowering, as they will feel directly connected to the outputs and outcomes of the organization.

---

[11] The other statements I have drafted personally and do not represent the school. As of the time of writing this book, I have not worked with the various teams in the school for a number of years. I also would not publish anything about a client that isn't already part of the public domain.

The more familiar staff are with the guiding statements of the school, as well as aligned to the guiding statements, the more diligently they will work to ensure those statements are realized. They will be intrinsically motivated and feel personally invested. Highly successful schools not only help personnel understand and measure the school's mission; they ensure teams define it in their own context and are aligned with it. This also supports why team leaders need to ensure personal interests in teams are aligned with the work that the team is doing. To achieve this, team members need to agree on the team's core purpose, and the team leader needs to ensure it aligns with the vision, mission, and strategic objectives of the school.

The protocol I facilitate to help teams agree on their core purpose is called "Establishing Purpose." Using this protocol for drafting statements of purpose at the core team level, with teams of four to eight people, can be developed within forty-five minutes, provided they have a common understanding of the school's vision, mission, and strategic objectives, and have successfully completed the previous forming activities. For larger groups, especially middle leadership teams or other heterogeneous teams, it may take two meetings to complete the statement of purpose. These more disparate teams need time to reflect on how others in the group perceive the purpose of the team, define their respective role in it, identify common interests, and allow the team leader to synthesize the statements. In the second meeting, the team leader presents what he or she felt encapsulated everyone's contribution and is aligned with the school's vision, mission, and strategic objectives.

For this activity, you will need pens, note-taking paper, chart paper, and felt-tip markers. The team's values, leadership characteristics, and group norms should be displayed (these are outputs from the previous chapter's activities), and the school's vision, mission, and strategic objectives should be reviewed. Make sure everyone comes to the meeting already familiar with the content and then give them a few minutes in the meeting to ensure they are focused on it. To ensure what team members draft is in their own words, remove or cover up the displayed content, then prompt them with these questions: "In respect to what our school seeks to achieve:

- Why does this team exist?

- What should we do in the time that we have together? and
- How will we do it?"

One vital aspect of my prompt is "in the time that we have together." The longer teams believe they will be together, the more ambitious their purpose should be. In some cases, though, grade-level and subject teams may be asked to achieve an outcome in a very short period, such as implementing significant curricular changes or changing their planning and assessment practices. Changes in curriculum and practice can impact a team's values, beliefs, and behaviors, completely consuming their time and attention, and should therefore be their primary focus for the year in which these changes take place. Learning community teams, committees, and departments should see themselves as having a more enduring presence and therefore should seek to achieve more ambitious outcomes.

After you have removed or covered the reference materials, write or display the prompt so it is visible to all team members. Instruct everyone that they have three minutes to draft what they feel should be the team's statement of purpose. Assure them that the output for this step should not be a beautifully crafted statement but ideas, bullet points, or sentences that address the why, what, and how. After three minutes, if everyone is still processing and writing, remind them of the time and give them two more minutes to finish. By the end of five minutes, everyone should have something they can present to a peer and discuss. At this time, pair team members up to share what they have written and give them five minutes to agree on what they feel the mission of the team should be. Working in pairs, they should be able to craft something more reminiscent of a statement of purpose, but it by no means needs to be complete, just something that represents their combined thoughts.

For a team of four to eight, each pair should present their synthesized statements of purpose. For teams of eight or more, engage in one more round where the pairs form groups of four and combine their statements. The importance of this process, when it comes time to agree on the core purpose of the team, is that iterations of building consensus have already taken place. Team members' perceptions of the purpose of the team will be less disparate and they will have already entered the process of having reached an agreement on core elements of the team's purpose. Additionally, in this last round, everyone will be excitedly sharing refined ideas. The facilitator's job at this time is to draft a statement of purpose while the team members are talking, something that uses language from the drafts of the smaller groups, as well as from the previous forming activities and school statements.

In addition to establishing purpose, this activity gives team members a platform and time to share beliefs and surface ideas about core purpose. By encouraging each team to draft a statement, it connects their values and beliefs with the team, which is the heart of transformational collaboration. Collectively, each statement of purpose will be aligned with the school, but specific to each team's context. This simple protocol will align individual team member thinking and interests within the team and ensure the work of the team contributes to the development of the school.

The importance of the team statement of purpose can't be stressed enough. A team getting derailed three to six months into the school year is highly probable. The cause for derailment can either be the inability to mitigate conflict or member divergence in pursuing the team goal. No matter the reason for derailment, if the team does not have a shared purpose to remind them of what they are working to achieve, they will eventually retreat to their classrooms, where they can focus on and achieve personal goals.

Make sure to avoid crafting broad statements, such as "We will improve student learning," because individual interpretations of how to achieve that purpose can be vastly different. In contrast, this statement is much more vivid and defines the work of the team: "To meet the needs of all learners, we will work interdependently to observe and provide feedback in our exploration of various differentiated learning strategies." This is not a goal, though. The goals that result from this statement should be more specific in terms of outputs, measurement, and time.

Unfortunately, school leadership has this misconception that there should only be one set of guiding statements for a school and that teams and individuals should only make goals. The flaw in having individual teams develop goals related to the school's more general and higher-level guiding statements is that without an interpretation of those statements in the context that the team works, the goals that they agree on will either be vague or self-serving. Some schools take steps to elaborate on the guiding statements, which then turn into a four-page flier about what the statements mean and the role each member of the community plays in achieving them. I would argue that the flier overcomplicates the purpose of the guiding statements, and furthermore makes it more difficult for all members of the community to connect with it. In fact, if the statement of purpose and/or goal is too specific, team performance is reduced, as evidenced by this quote from Jennifer D. Nahrgang:

> "SPECIFIC LEARNING GOALS IN TEAMS FOCUS INDIVIDUALS' ATTENTION ON NARROW ELEMENTS OF THEIR TASKS, THUS REDUCING COORDINATION, COMMUNICATION AND TEAMWORK–RESULTING IN MISSED OPPORTUNITIES FOR LEARNING AND INNOVATION."
> — NAHRGANG ET AL., ORGANIZATIONAL BEHAVIOR AND HUMAN DECISION PROCESSES, 2013

With this in mind, and given the efficacious nature of educators, the goal-setting process can be self-serving if team leaders aren't critical of how the goals contribute to the desired outcome. Engaging in transactional goals does not contribute to improving student learning in the long term, and any gains won't be sustainable, especially if the team experiences any change in composition. Additionally, if teams, as well as individuals, pursue vastly different and unrelated goals, the opportunity to scale the effect of the outputs for those goals is lost. Lastly, provisioning resources, such a budget for professional development for individuals and teams, is spread thin, which greatly reduces the potential impact of those resources.

Although we have tackled the most time-consuming, and taken-for-granted, forming activities, we still aren't out of the Forming Stage. The team needs to establish goals, clarify each team member's role respective to those goals, and agree on processes for planning and decision-making. All of this happens in parallel with life and individual work responsibilities, hence the Forming Stage takes two to three months to complete and why goals should be established at the end of the Forming Stage.

Secondary outcomes for the activities completed up to this point have been the following:

1. Team members understand, and have experienced, how their values and beliefs are similar and how to appropriately communicate their differences;
2. Team members have been exposed to a way of communicating beliefs that focus on the work of the team;
3. Team members learned how to build consensus, which meant compromising and focusing on what's most important and aligning with the team;
4. Team members had the opportunity to model, practice, and reinforce effective communication;
5. The team leader facilitated an effective team process for building consensus, which was to ensure:
    - At the start of all activities, team members had time to form their own thoughts, in silence;
    - Equal time was given to all team members to share those thoughts;
    - For larger teams, a consensus was built through scaffolding discussions with smaller groups building consensus and then speaking as one voice to synthesize their ideas with other small groups;
6. Roles were assigned for documenting and summarizing key ideas and information; and
7. The team produced an output—a win.

In the next chapter, we will further explore how to replicate this process in meetings, as well as how to scale this process for more significant and potentially contentious topics.

This now concludes the first workshop I spoke of in Lecture 7. You might be able to complete all the forming activities in the team's first meeting, but the team should still plan to make time to familiarize themselves with what they have agreed upon, and they may wish to further clarify norms or further edit their statement of purpose. During this period, the team leader's job is to ensure the team is engaging in dialogue that further clarifies what they have surfaced and defines their roles and responsibilities as they relate to the team. For the next workshop, which usually takes place three to four weeks later, I ask participants to bring their team's agreed-upon norms and statement of purpose. These are essential for facilitating purposeful meetings.

Before I proceed to effective meeting management, I want to bring closure to how to align goals with the team mission, as well as the role of inquiry to drive the process. Often, as a homework assignment, I will facilitate an activity that produces a leadership inquiry for each participant. The objective is for me to better understand what participants want to get from the course, but it is also intended to introduce them to the skills of developing effective inquiries that will guide their own learning and leadership development. As stated earlier in this book, leadership is not something learned in a class or a book. It begins with a problem you want to solve, and that problem is in the form of a question. When we answer that question, we grow as leaders. Setting goals is a similar process.

CHAPTER 10
FACILITATING PURPOSEFUL MEETINGS

The first workshop activities (Chapters 8 and 9), which I recommend being done in your first meeting, have predictable outputs that contribute to a tangible outcome, a shared purpose. However, if the team is not afforded the luxury of three to four hours to engage in these activities when they first meet, they will need to agree to put them at the beginning of the agendas for subsequent meetings. The activities and the purpose of the activities should be introduced in the first meeting, though.

This, in essence, is effective meeting management; participants know why they are meeting, what they are doing in the meeting,
how they should prepare, and what the output of the meeting should be. These activities also reinforce effective facilitation in that participants are given equal opportunities to contribute, and their contributions are the foundation for building consensus and making decisions together.

Meeting Attribute	Effective Meetings	Ineffective Meetings
Planning	- Transactional work is done outside the meeting - Team members are aware of how to prepare - Personal issues are addressed before the meeting - Planning is flexible	- *Ad hoc* Agendas - Schedule dictated by the school calendar - Discussion dominated by some team members - The agenda can't accommodate unplanned events
Purposeful	- The purpose of agenda topics is clear - Team purpose and norms are visible on the agenda - Discussions are summarized, relevant decisions are documented and roles and deadlines clarified	- Team members leave the meeting uncertain of what they are supposed to do and when - Norms aren't enforced - Lack of equity for discussion time
Debriefing	- The team reviews their norms and team purpose regularly - Team norms evolve to encourage collaborative communication	- Elephants aren't addressed - An endless stream of tasks with no time to celebrate

Facilitator	• Makes norms and purpose of meeting explicit • Assertively facilitates meetings • Ensures equity • Develops team members' facilitative capacity	• Allows team members to dominate the discussion • Doesn't mitigate conflict • Doesn't demonstrate agreed-upon leadership attributes
Roles	• Team members share responsibility for administrative tasks (agendas, minutes, and school announcements) • Timekeepers • Minute takers	• The team leader is expected to do all communications and team administration • Team members only contribute when they are interested

Planning

Team leaders in schools are often chosen because of their technical skills, or, in some cases, because it's "their turn to lead." They haven't had any orientation to their role, let alone training on how to manage what is arguably the largest part of their job, facilitating team meetings. I seldom meet teacher leaders who are cognizant of what is expected of them from senior leaders, let alone from their peers, in terms of how to lead a meeting. Often, there is neither a policy for meeting management, let alone an agenda template to help them organize. The expectation for this most critical responsibility is shaped by the team leader's own experiences, whether bad or good, and usually is planned around transactional agenda items.

Meetings are a school's most commonly used, and abused, tool for collaboration. The school's master calendar also sets the expectation that people have to meet, regardless of the time together is used effectively. Meetings in this instance won't be very inclusive and the agendas often *ad hoc*. *Ad hoc* agendas are often the result of the team leader using the meeting to "organize" or catch up with team members. These meetings will fail to connect with team members' values and beliefs and will be seen as burdensome. The team leader will feel compelled to enforce the meeting time and team members will be resentful. Ultimately, any work the team must produce will lack buy-in as to who should do what how it should be done, and the work of the team will fall to one or a few individuals.

Most meetings, unfortunately, take place because they are mandated, the common planning period meeting. However, these meetings often devolve into disseminating information and checking in on individual tasks. These informational or check-in meetings are usually a result of team leaders being caught between two factions: senior leaders needing reassurance that people are doing their job and team members needing clarification on what is expected of them. Amazingly enough, since most meeting time is spent sharing information, most of the transactional work teams accomplish is done outside the meetings, individually and not interdependently.

Weekly forty- to sixty-minute meetings should be sufficient for teams to engage in more meaningful and interdependent work. In order to capacity-build team leaders to become more effective, team leaders need time to plan and coordinate, and they need good facilitation skills. The former ensures that when the team meets, they have a purpose, and the latter ensures the team stays focused during the meeting.

I often tell my workshop participants that even though they may meet once a week for forty to sixty minutes, to ensure that the meeting is effective, it should actually be the culmination of two to three hours of planning and coordination activities. Leaders that invest the time to ensure the work of the team is purposeful will benefit by having team members who are more engaged with the work of the team. During the two to three hours of planning and coordination, several of the transactional items that take up meeting time will also be attended to, such as checking in on tasks that team members are meant to report on.

Given time to plan and coordinate, team leaders can ensure their members are given an agenda and relevant materials to review in advance. Questions and comments can be dealt with before the meeting. The meeting itself won't become an excuse to plan or negotiate the demands of competing factions. Agenda items requiring time for processing or reflection can be dealt with outside the meeting, especially considering that each team member will process information differently. Members will come to meetings having already thought through the discussion points and prepared to contribute.

Poorly planned meetings will end up with one or a few members dominating the conversation as they quickly react to agenda items, regardless of if the actions proposed or feedback given is in the best interest of the whole group. This perpetuates an atmosphere of passivity among less outspoken members. These meetings tend to only end in agreement on how to achieve transactional goals, as input is limited and opportunities to connect beliefs to practice are not given adequate consideration.

Team leaders need to also accept and prepare for some agendas being doomed to fail, as emergencies and competing initiatives within the school will hijack team meetings, thus squeezing out time for transformative work. These outside influences, in addition to team members being late or not prepared, will eat away at the agenda and reduce the effectiveness of meetings. These factors can be debilitating to team leadership and further dissuade team leaders from trying to accomplish anything more than transactional goals. The will to do something transformative diminishes.

Other examples of poor meeting planning are "check-in" and "school policy" meetings. These are unnecessary evils, as they can be done virtually. The reason these meetings are mandated is that senior leaders and team leaders don't trust staff to read emails and newsletters. This distrust is reinforced by staff not replying with relevant responses, or by emails being deprioritized and only attended to when people are reminded. Hence, it is easier to make everyone meet as opposed to trusting they will take the desired actions.

One solution to rectifying this would be using technology, in the same way that online service providers send us numerous emails updating their terms and conditions. Or whenever we visit a new website, we must accept its content use policy. As soon as we open the email or click the accept button on the use policy, we are acknowledging receipt and acceptance of the information. Schools could similarly track staff to look for trends in who is responding to announcements in a timely manner and differentiate its approach to those that aren't. Those that aren't responding could be called into meetings before or after school. This solution would ensure that meeting time is protected for purposeful work.

Senior leaders and team leaders are aware of what can disrupt their meeting planning, but for some reason, they often fail to plan for these obstacles. The mentality is to hope for the best, and if anything goes wrong, they either persevere by focusing on transactional agenda items or they push the more meaningful agenda items to another meeting. The danger with these two results is that team members will never get to talk about issues that matter to them. Soon, meetings are perceived as punishments, in that members will associate meetings with more time-consuming, unrewarding work.

For this reason, both senior leaders and team leaders need to be flexible in their planning. Not only do meeting agendas need to have buffers, but there needs to be time to process what is happening in the surrounding community and understand how that will affect the work of the team.

Purposeful

To ensure meetings are purposeful we need to understand the purpose of the meeting. Christine Comaford described three types of meetings in a Forbes Magazine article, "*3 Types Of Meetings That Will Engage Your Team And Increase Team Performance.*" This image illustrates the 3 types of meetings relative to the frequency that they should occur and the time for desirable debate during each meeting.

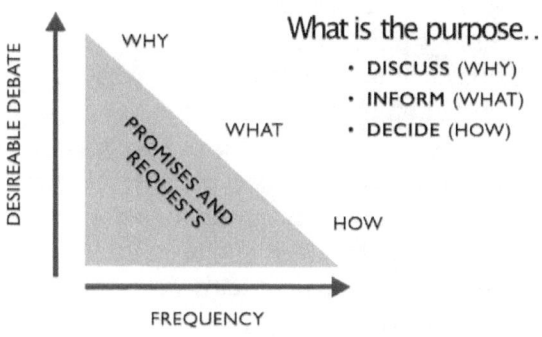

Debriefing and Forming activity meetings are good examples of *why* meetings. In these meetings, teams are surfacing values and beliefs and establishing or reaffirming vision and strategy. *Why* meetings are characterized by longer periods of debate, but meeting less frequently. The reason for this is that once the purpose has been established and bought into, teams can begin focusing on the work to be done.

What meetings are for frontloading, ensuring all team members have a common understanding of what needs to be done and engaging in ideation. *What* meeting agenda items focus on clarifying roles, responsibilities and expected outcomes. These meetings also may experience the greatest amount of conflict, hence why there needs to be more time for debate, as well as a greater frequency of meetings.

Planning meetings are for deciding *how* the team will proceed and monitoring the team's progress. These meetings are more for reporting and ensuring alignment between team members that have reciprocal interdependencies. *How* meetings give team members an opportunity to collaboratively problem solve and broaden perspective on different approaches to completing their work.

Each type of meeting has specific agenda items and these items have predictable results. For example, any agenda item that purposefully addresses *why* will take a long time to facilitate, as it provokes team members to surface their values and requires full participation to achieve buy-in. *What* meetings are opportunities to ensure a common understanding of the issues affecting the team and help the team to identify obstacles that they can subsequently prepare for. *How* meetings, should ensure alignment and reinforce the importance of working interdependently.

All these meetings ultimately culminate in promises or requests for action based on the discussions being properly summarized and actions to be reported on in the next meeting. These actions may be the need to answer additional questions or take specific actions that result in progress towards the stated purpose of the team. Team members walk away from these meetings knowing what needs to be done, who will do it and when it is supposed to be done. With this level of clarity, and expectations explicitly made clear, the next most important meeting, debriefing, will be a welcome respite from the endless streams of work.

Debriefing

One significant obstacle to achieving transformational collaboration, where the meeting is vital, is time to debrief work as a team. Transactional goals don't require debriefing; they are either done or not done. If not done, we quickly identify obstacles and delegate accordingly. Transformational collaboration, however, requires time to debrief. The pulse of the team needs to be taken, and difficult conversations need to be facilitated. Not every meeting requires time set aside to debrief, though. Debriefing is not an opportunity to check in; it comes at various stages of team development and at the completion of significant goal milestones. When debriefing team development and goal milestones, it should be the only item on the agenda, as these meetings are opportunities for team members to surface concerns about how the team works. These meetings mitigate conflict and reaffirm buy-in to the team's purpose. The longer these meetings are put off, the more likely that team members will become less engaged.

Academic teams that run on a fixed school calendar should be debriefing their work as a team every two to three months. Debrief meetings should answer four essential questions, relative to their agreed-upon purpose:

1. What have we achieved to date?
   (An opportunity to celebrate)

2. What are we doing well as a team that we need to keep doing?
   (An opportunity to celebrate)

3. What should we be doing more of to achieve our stated purpose?
   (An opportunity to review norms and team processes)

4. What should our focus be for the next two months?
   (An opportunity to set short terms goals to help with performance management)

These questions not only provide a safe environment to surface critical feedback, but they are scaffolded in such a way as to build energy in a meeting and ensure there is closure at the end by identifying concrete actions. Additionally, these meetings are an opportunity to reassess team goals and group norms.

Taking time to reflect on team goals should be a reward, in that this is the reason people have invested in the team. These goals are reflective of their values and beliefs. Taking time to evaluate the team's performance relative to their goals is an opportunity to focus conversations on practice and talk about what's going on in the classroom, which is probably the most desired conversation topic among educators but one they seldom get to engage in. Debriefing team goals gives everyone a chance to share research and experience. Not only do team members get to take a lead role in these meetings, but they walk away with a feeling of having been professionally developed.

In the case of norms, as the team grows and becomes more engaged in each other's practice, the behaviors they need to be mindful of will change. The team needs to move from a state of self-awareness to being aware of others. We will discuss these states in more detail in the next chapter, but a simple example of this would be: At the beginning of the school year, or the Forming Stage, a group norm many teams need is for team members to come prepared to contribute. Transactional norms are needed at the beginning of the school year, such as be on time, come prepared and use technology appropriately. Within three months, teams should have mastered these norms by demonstrating they can hold each other accountable to them. At this point, during a debriefing meeting, you can evaluate what norms can be removed and replace them with transformative norms.

During the Storming Stage, team members need to move beyond transactional norms and begin focusing on transformative norms, such as asking team members to assume positive intent; be understanding of others' intentions. One very important note, you can't ask team members to adhere to transformative norms if people are coming late to meetings, being unprepared, or replying to emails during meetings. Do not take the transactional norms for granted; master them early and use them as a quick win in your first debriefing meeting.

Not only will these meetings serve to re-evaluate group norms, but the team should assess if agreed-upon goals are still relevant. As a team develops and the school year progresses, the context that necessitated the original goal may no longer be relevant. In some cases, some goals may have been too general or vague and the debrief meeting is an opportunity to further refine the goal. Also, values influence beliefs and beliefs influence behaviors. Goals and behaviors have a reciprocal effect on each other. Therefore, as the team matures and experiences new types of conflict, arising from pursuing a goal, they need to modify different behaviors to mitigate conflict. This is true of reassessing goals as well, because as the team moves into a more transformative state, they should be emboldened to seek more transformative goals.

Facilitator

To be an effective meeting facilitator, you need to ensure your participants are entering the meeting with a clear understanding of the expected output. Defining meetings as *why*, *what*, or *how* is a simple and effective tool when there is a common understanding of the definitions for these meetings and what outputs they typically produce. Once established, you need to stay true to the intent of these meetings. An example of how a meeting purpose is undermined is when *how* meetings are used for the team leader to check in to ensure each person has finished grading or unit planning or has completed some administrative task.

Team meetings are about the team; therefore, a good example of a *how* meeting is one that requires team members to report on work that informs the team of the challenges or progress of individual members working toward a team goal, such that other members can learn from that experience. In *how* meetings, team members should be collaboratively problem-solving and sharing experiences that benefit the team.

The next most important thing to remember to be an effective and influential meeting facilitator is to ensure that meetings are always purposeful and that people leave the meeting with the feeling that they have contributed to the team's development. This is achieved when we structure meetings to ensure equity and finish meetings with well-defined promises or requests for action. To ensure meetings are purposeful, the team's statement of purpose should be at the top of every agenda. Every agenda item and any decisions made should support that statement of purpose. To ensure equity, the team's norms should be visible in every meeting, with the facilitator identifying one norm at the beginning of the meeting that they want everyone to be conscious of during the meeting. This ensures that everyone will remain aware of themselves and other[12] throughout the meeting.

The team's statement of purpose and norms are incredibly powerful facilitation tools. When crafted correctly, they are representative of the values and beliefs of all team members. When off-topic discussions erupt in meetings, ones that don't support the team's stated purpose, or when team members behave contrary to the agreed-upon norms, the facilitator has the power to invoke the collective will of the team to get the meeting back on track. In exceptional cases, though, a good facilitator will end a meeting if a discussion or norms infraction threatens any member of the team. A good facilitator will also question whether a meeting is necessary and should cancel meetings if the agenda items to be addressed don't attend to the needs of all members. This puts an additional burden on the team leader, but it is a great way to build goodwill early on in a school year.

To ensure meetings stay on topic and are equitable can take a lot of energy and use up a lot of relationship capital. However, provided the meeting chair is assertive and stays focused on achieving the stated objective of the meeting, they can overcome the most difficult of meeting personalities. The key is to be assertive, which can easily be confused with being authoritative. But the main difference is that an assertive speaker has the:

1. RIGHT THINKING
2. RIGHT LANGUAGE
3. RIGHT BEHAVIOR

Facilitation is largely a communication skill. It does require planning and coordination, but to be an effective facilitator, you need to be a good communicator. You need to know when and how to

---

[12] In Chapter 11, the Experience Cube is introduced as an activity to help team members develop the capability to be aware of their own thoughts and feelings during meetings, as well as how to become aware of and understand the thoughts and feelings of other team members.

interject yourself into discussions. You need to be able to paraphrase and pause effectively. To communicate effectively, you need to be confident; this requires the *right thinking*. As the meeting facilitator, you have been entrusted with the responsibility of ensuring the meeting is purposeful and that all participants walk away feeling a sense of accomplishment. To do this, you need to trust that you are the caretaker of the team's norms and mission. When discussions or behaviors conflict with the norms or mission, it is *your right* to address those infractions on behalf of all team members.

When you invoke that right, you need to use the *right language*. When the time comes to interject in a heated discussion or if you need to interrupt someone, you do it by stating what you are observing and how you feel it may impact achieving the objective of the meeting. When you have the *right thinking* and use the *right language*, your body should express the *right behavior*, in that it should be calm and non-aggressive.

Ideally, all team members should have this skill, but often what happens is that a well-meaning discussion can devolve into personal experience–sharing or point-proving. If team members still feel their point or experience is valid, then a good facilitator will remind them of the time left for discussion and ensure they connect the point or experience to the meeting's objective. If meeting participants are unable to do this, it is either because they have come to the meeting unprepared or because new information has provoked a new line of thought. In both cases, that team member should be encouraged to develop that thought outside the meeting and be allowed to share it in the next meeting.

Although being a good meeting facilitator is the hallmark of a good team leader, the ability to develop this skill in all team members is what makes for a *great* team leader. Team leaders should capacity-build the facilitation skills of the whole team. When policing behavior or directing discussions back to the mission of the team becomes the work of only one person, it is often indicative of only that one person being bought into the work of the team. The good news is once you have completed all the forming activities, you are well on your way to capacity-building each team member's facilitation skills. Each forming activity is meant to not only ensure buy-in, but also instill a degree of accountability in each team member. The ability to switch a team member from being a passive supporter of the team norms and purpose to a full-fledged vocal advocate is largely a matter of delegating team leadership responsibilities to them.

As noted above, successful facilitation relies on being assertive, and to be assertive you need to have the right thinking. If team members are bought into and believe in the team processes, then they are halfway to becoming vocal advocates. The remaining journey toward developing their facilitation skills lies in the relationship they have with each team member and the type of leadership tasks they feel comfortable assuming.

Roles

To begin capacity-building team members' facilitation skills, first focus on getting them to assume responsibility for various administrative responsibilities related to the team. This suggestion is often met with great skepticism but once implemented it is found to be overwhelmingly successful. The most successful way to achieve this is to delegate agenda-setting and meeting facilitation to team members. Encourage team members to take responsibility for checking in with other team members on various tasks, for example, one team member can be responsible for ensuring everyone understands the lesson planning template and another team member can be responsible for helping team members with student reports.

To prepare team members for facilitating meetings, you need to strengthen interdependency among team members by having them work in pairs or larger groups to research and report on topics that they have a keen interest in and that are beneficial to the work of the team. Ensure the reports provide guidance on how team members can use the new information to improve their own practices and have the presenters follow up with other team members to see how they are using the new information or, potentially, what obstacles they are encountering that the presenters can do further research on. Once team members demonstrate they are comfortable reporting to and supporting team members, begin to delegate whole meetings to different team members.

The reason this suggestion is often met with skepticism is that, in some cases, team members may openly challenge such delegation as trying to offload leadership duties the team leader is compensated for, but in many cases, it is the team leader who is worried that they will be seen as trying to offload those duties. If the forming activities are successfully completed and reinforced, then team members will appreciate that they all have an equal part in ensuring the success of the team. The team leader's job is to orchestrate the work of the team, which requires a great amount of energy and resources. Once team members assume greater responsibility for the management of team processes, the team leader is freed up to spend more time on identifying and acquiring resources for the team, which includes building a network to manage upward.

A reasonable expectation for when a team leader could begin to delegate management tasks to team members would be at the end of the Storming Stage, about three months after the completion of the forming activities. The reason for this is because during these initial three months, things that seemed clear in the beginning become very unclear once initial steps are taken. Also, many competing tasks and initiatives begin to surface during this time that distract team members and cause them to question priorities.

The norms and purpose of the team will be tested repeatedly during this period of adjustment, as the team enters the Storming Stage. I call it a period of adjustment because the team needs to settle into a new normal and adjust how they individually work to accommodate how the team works. The team leader's role during this period is to focus on relationships and ensure every meeting is purposeful. This not only keeps team members focused on the work of the team, but also demonstrates effective facilitation skills.

During this period, the team leader needs to be aware of five distinct and potentially disrupting behaviors. If the team leader can assertively mitigate the potential for disruption from these behaviors, they will ensure a safe space for team members to develop their own leadership capacity. In the next chapter, I will identify strategies for how to mitigate these behaviors in meetings, but, more important, I will explain why we need to avoid labelling team members by attributing their behavior to their character.

CHAPTER 11

COLLABORATIVE COMMUNICATION

> "WHEN TEACHERS COLLABORATE, THEY RUN HEADLONG INTO ENORMOUS CONFLICTS OVER PROFESSIONAL BELIEFS AND PRACTICES. IN THEIR OPTIMISM ABOUT CARING AND SUPPORTIVE COMMUNITIES, ADVOCATES OFTEN UNDERPLAY THE ROLE OF DIVERSITY, DISSENT, AND DISAGREEMENT IN COMMUNITY LIFE, LEAVING PRACTITIONERS ILL-PREPARED AND CONCEPTIONS OF COLLABORATION UNDEREXPLORED."
> — ACHINSTEIN, 2002

Every time I facilitate the Implicit Leadership Theory forming activity, without fail, communication skills are the most highly desired attribute of a great leader. The communication skills commonly referenced range from general, such as communicates clearly to something more specific, such as active listener. The most empowering experience for a team member is that of being heard and having what is communicated back to them address their need. Often, the most pressing need is clarity on the question, "What do you want me to do?"

When team members are clear about what is expected of them and the team, feel listened to and understand what actions need to be taken, they will demonstrate behaviors that positively reinforce transformational collaboration. Team members will ensure equity in terms of discussion time and contributions to the team, as well as prioritize teamwork and meetings ahead of personal priorities. Team members, more importantly, will collaboratively communicate and demonstrate the Seven Norms of Collaboration.

When team members feel that they are not being listened to and that what is being communicated to them is not addressing their needs, they will demonstrate behaviors in meetings that undermine collaboration. These undermining behaviors, or what I refer to as difficult behaviors, often originate from:

1. Norms not being enforced,
2. Those affected by norm infractions attributing behaviors they deem difficult to a team member's character, and
3. Team members not being able to appropriately express their own thoughts and feelings.

5 Difficult Behaviors

Five common behaviors that undermine collaboration and are often observed in meetings, are:

NAYSAYING	Those who reflexively disagree with the suggestions of others.
AGGRESSIVE	Those who express disagreement inappropriately.
DOMINATING	Those who dominate discussions with redundant or unnecessarily long responses.
ATTENTION-SEEKING	Those who feel the need to be the focal point at meetings.
AVOIDING	Those who cannot or will not focus at meetings.

These are observable behaviors, so let's quickly dispel by attributing the behaviors to the character of the person exhibiting these behaviors, or, in other words, labelling these behaviors as personality traits. It's easy to observe these behaviors and develop an untested narrative about the person displaying these behaviors that will color all future interactions between yourself and that person. These behaviors, as mentioned in the last chapter, begin to surface in the Storming Stage, when the team is beginning to pursue its goals.

When these behaviors surface in meetings, they will disrupt the work of the team and, if allowed to persist, will cause team members to disengage from the work of the team completely. The opening quote from Betty Achinstein sums up precisely why these behaviors surface early; largely, they are born of optimism and caring. In some cases, team members are eager to contribute, but may not be aware of how their interaction with other team members is being perceived. In other cases, they may worry their behavior will cause conflict and then hold back or withdraw from the team. They lack awareness of each other.

An example of this would be someone always eager to contribute crowding out the ability for others to speak. This person quickly could be labelled as dominating. Their good intentions can quickly turn sour if they feel team members are ignoring them and they are incapable of influencing their peers. There is also the potential risk, if the "personality" is unaddressed, that it will persist through the remainder of the school year. The flip side to this scenario would be if that same team member, aware of their tendency to dominate discussions, senses the will of the team may not align with their own beliefs and practices, may demonstrate avoidance behaviors to avoid being the center of conflict.

Let's first reflect on some strategies that directly address these behaviors so that they don't become "elephants in the room." The expression the **elephant in the room** is a metaphorical idiom in English for an important or an obvious major problem or issue that people avoid discussing or acknowledging. When these difficult behaviors surface in meetings, they must be addressed. How the behaviors are addressed is dependent on time and place. The most important time and place consideration is the stage of development the team is in. If relationships and trust are still forming, addressing behaviors directly can be unsettling not only to those exhibiting the behavior but also to those who witness the addressing.

Below is a list of strategies for addressing each behavior. Each strategy has a time and place it will be most effective. The suggestions are ordered based on the stage of development the team is in, with the first strategy being the least direct and the last strategy being the most direct.

NAYSAYING:
- Ask the naysayer what alternatives he or she would propose
- Ask the naysayer, "What would have to change for the proposed solution to work?" Do not accept "It won't work" as a response.
- Ask the group for opinions on the naysayer's comments

AGGRESSIVE:
- Remind them to limit comments to ideas rather than people
- Refer to the staff's agreed-upon norms of behavior for meetings
- If the aggressor's comment is not directed at an individual, ignore it until the break, when you can speak privately
- If the statement is made directly to you, be professional and respectful. Acknowledge that there are different ways to think about any given topic. Avoid becoming defensive or getting drawn into an argument.
- Ask other participants if they agree with the aggressor's statements

DOMINATING:
- Break eye contact and call on someone else by name
- Impose a time limit on all staff members' responses
- When the dominator pauses for breath, take the opportunity to ask for someone else's opinion
- Visibly post a flip chart at the beginning of every meeting and label it "Parking Lot." Use sticky notes to write down his or her comment on the sticky note and place it on the flip chart. At the end of the meeting, review the comments.
- Make a non-verbal gesture to interrupt the dominator

ATTENTION SEEKING:
- Ask attention seekers to help with tasks such as note taking
- If the attention-seeking behavior is not disruptive, ignore it (e.g., by turning your back to the attention seeker)
- Ask them to chair a meeting, including setting the agenda and ensuring everyone comes prepared.

AVOIDING:
- Start meetings on time and with engaging activities
- Have avoiders catch up with you after the meeting
- Arrange the physical environment so that you can always make eye contact with all staff members.
- When avoiders engage in side conversations, walk toward them casually while continuing to lead the meeting, then stand near them until they cease talking.
- When a team member appears reluctant to participate in a large group activity, address him or her directly.

Enforcing Norms

With a few strategies in hand, let's now take a step back and consider how these behaviors manifest and, more important, become the norm for behavior in meetings. Jeffrey T. Polzer (2003) found that the very first team meeting often becomes the norm for how teams operate. In the context of a team that does not enforce group norms and tries to stay focused on transactional work, they begin reinforcing implicit norms for transactional collaboration and reinforce what Hargreaves and Dawe (1990) call *contrived collegiality*. In 1994 Andy Hargreaves introduced six identifying characteristics of contrived collegiality, which I believe are also indicative of a transactional culture:

- Administratively regulated,
- Compulsory,
- Implementation-oriented,
- Fixed in space
- Fixed in time, and
- Predictable.

The difference between transactional and transformational behavioral norms is quite large. In a transactional culture, we only care about what has been done. To ensure we stay on top of our tasks, we ask team members to do the following:

1. Be prepared for meetings,
2. Come on time,

3. Report on tasks assigned to each team member, and

4. Contribute to the work of the team.

These are just examples of the types of behavioral norms that teams agree to when they are primarily transaction-focused, such as completing lesson and unit plans, turning in grades and reports on time, etc.

In a transformational culture, we care more about the substance and depth of interaction with our team members. In order to benefit from each other's knowledge, experience, and interests, we need to, for the most part, transition the team to being aware of and demonstrating the Seven Norms for Collaboration. These norms make team members more mindful of self and other when engaging in meaningful dialogue. However, to achieve this level of awareness, and to demonstrate these norms effectively, requires a great amount of trust and respect.

This said, to earn that trust and respect, the best place to start is with demonstrating transactional excellence, i.e., being prepared and on time for meetings, volunteering to assist colleagues with planning and preparation, and demonstrating a keen interest in what team members have to say. As discussed previously, to get to transformational norms, you most likely need to work through transactional norms. There is no point in having active listening as a norm if people are late to meetings or searching unrelated topics on their laptop during discussions. As discussed in the last chapter, to evolve beyond transactional norms, you need to take time to debrief, assess, and refine team processes.

Furthermore, to hold team members accountable to these norms requires strong facilitation skills, as was discussed in Chapter 10. Often, team leaders will opt to not address the difficult behaviors in a meeting and will say that the behavior is best addressed in private outside the meeting. Two problems with this reasoning are that by not addressing the behavior in the meeting, you are signaling to other team members that the behavior is acceptable. Second, the difficult conversation to address the behavior is often never had, which signals to the person exhibiting the behavior that it is acceptable, therefore reinforcing it. Additionally, a behavior that goes unaddressed becomes much more difficult to address later, as you lose the power to reference agreed-upon norms. By not having reinforced the will of the team early on, later attempts to address difficult behaviors will be perceived as personal criticisms.

Experience Cube

Even more damaging to the team, when difficult behaviors are not addressed, is that team members observing the behavior will begin forming their own narrative about the person demonstrating the behavior. When these behaviors surface, it is easy to attribute them to the character of the person and label that person as a difficult person, from which the person developing this narrative can fall into a reflexive loop where they become more acutely aware of, and focus solely on, the difficult behaviors and attribute those behaviors to the team member's character. Once the team member has been labelled, all future interactions with them are colored by that label. Regardless of if their intention is positive, what they communicate will be perceived inaccurately.

This is also a reciprocal process. As Team Member A, the person who is developing the narrative about the "difficult person," demonstrates behaviors consistent with their beliefs about Team Member B, the "difficult person," Team Member B will either feel more justified in demonstrating the difficult behaviors so as to be heard or both team members will withdraw from the team completely and take more passive-aggressive stances toward any future teamwork. Unfortunately, Team Member B may have adopted inappropriate communication strategies because it was the only way they felt heard and were able to influence team members. This belief also most likely predates the existing team, in which case the behaviors demonstrated by Team Member B were the norm on a previous team.

HIDDEN IN PLAIN SIGHT

This concept of personal narrative is supported by what Chris Argyris called the *Ladder of Inference* [13], a common mental pathway of increasing abstraction, often leading to misguided beliefs:

> "WE LIVE IN A WORLD OF SELF-GENERATING BELIEFS, WHICH REMAIN LARGELY UNTESTED. WE ADOPT THOSE BELIEFS BECAUSE THEY ARE BASED ON CONCLUSIONS, WHICH ARE INFERRED FROM WHAT WE OBSERVE, PLUS OUR PAST EXPERIENCE. OUR ABILITY TO ACHIEVE THE RESULTS WE TRULY DESIRE IS ERODED BY OUR FEELINGS THAT: OUR BELIEFS ARE THE TRUTH; THE TRUTH IS OBVIOUS; OUR BELIEFS ARE BASED ON REAL DATA; AND THE DATA WE SELECT ARE THE REAL DATA."
>
> – THE FIFTH DISCIPLINE FIELDBOOK. (1994)
> BY PETER M. SENGE, ART KLEINER, CHARLOTTE ROBERTS,
> RICHARD B. ROSS, AND BRYAN J. SMITH.

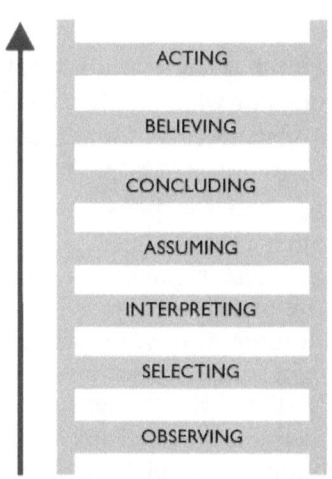

The Ladder of Inference has seven rungs, or the mental pathway, through which people make untested assumptions about others based on observations and past experience. These rungs are observable at the very bottom and top of the ladder, and all the rungs in between

---

[13] The Ladder of Inference was first put forward by organizational psychologist Chris Argyris and used by Peter Senge in *The Fifth Discipline: The Art and Practice of the Learning Organization*.

often occur without our awareness. The mental pathway through which we create these self-generating beliefs begins at the bottom, where we begin by observing data, or what we sense as "facts." From there, we:

- SELECTING - Select data based on our beliefs and prior experience.
- INTERPRETING - Interpret what they mean.
- ASSUMING - Create assumptions, often untested
- CONCLUDING - Make conclusions based on our assumptions.
- BELIEVING - Adopt beliefs supported by these conclusions.
- ACTING - Take actions based on what we believe.

In some cases, we may jump to conclusions by attributing observations directly to conclusions or what is otherwise known as a leap of abstraction. These leaps of abstraction forgo interpreting what we have observed. Assumptions go untested by not looking for additional data, for example speaking with the person we are observing to understand why they exhibited a behavior.

The reflexive loop, the most vicious part of this ladder that fuels negative narratives of others, occurs when our *beliefs* affect the *selected reality*. To put it more simply, we purposely observe data that reinforces our existing beliefs. Furthermore, between the rungs of "Selected Reality" and "Beliefs," the thought processes happen so quickly and in such imperceptible areas of our brain that people are unaware of how their emotions or actions are being affected by this process. In other words, the visible components of this ladder are run through processes that are unseen and unquestioned and the conclusions drawn are untested, leading to a poorly written narrative.

All hope is not lost, though. There are ways to unravel this invisible and self-perpetuating process and make it transparent. The first tool I will introduce is meant to build greater awareness of self and other in terms of the behaviors we are predisposed to exhibit, based on our work experience and the strategies we have adopted to be successful in our work environment. The second tool is based on the research by Gervase Bushe, specifically his Experience Cube (2009), which is a tool for structuring communication to ensure the Ladder of Inference becomes transparent.

The first tool is to use workplace behavioral assessments. There are several of these in the market that range from free to very expensive. The cost is often representative of the report produced by doing the assessments; those that are free are generally self-scoring and provide generic introductions to the results yielded. An example of a free behavioral assessment, which many educators may be familiar with, is *Compass Points*. This activity can be easily found online by searching for "Compass Points Work Behaviors" and can be completed in forty-five minutes. It doesn't provide any direction or insight into how to use what is learned from the activity, hence it is free. This activity has a greater impact on larger audiences, preferably over sixteen people and can be a great team-building activity.

Compass Points, like other tools for creating awareness about personality, categorizes people into profiles, in this case, North, South, East, and West. The premise for the activity, like other more sophisticated assessments, is to draw attention to the fact that people have different behavioral preferences, and these preferences dictate how they work and communicate with others. The four behavioral types, when not made explicit, can easily conflict with each other. For example, Northerners—I count myself as one—are defined as being direct and predisposed to take action, whereas Southerners are defined as demonstrating greater empathy and are less likely to take action. The conflict, in this case, is obvious to see, but if both people are aware of the other's behavioral tendencies, they can adapt their behavior and communication to be more effective at working with one another. More to this point, by these behavioral preferences being made explicit, team members can create more accurate narratives about their colleagues.

Two other workplace behavioral assessments that I commonly see in schools, especially when wanting to improve collaboration in teamwork-based environments and situations, is *DiSC (Dominance, Influence, Steadiness, and Compliance)* and *Myers–Briggs Type Indicator (MBTI)*. I favor DiSC for teaching, administrative, and governance teams, largely because the reports are much easier to understand and the strategies for improving collaboration and communication between the four profiles much easier to access and implement.

MBTI categorizes behavioral preferences into sixteen profile types. While the accuracy and depth of analysis can be greater with MBTI, ensuring the terminology and profile types are reinforced in the day-to-day communication of the working environment is much more difficult to achieve. Synthesizing the terminology and profile types into the working language is incredibly important. Being able to easily access and use the terminology is what ultimately determines the level of awareness people have of self and other. With DiSC, you are either a D (Dominance), an i (Influence), an S (Steadiness), or a C (Compliance). With MBTI you are one of sixteen combinations of eight different letters; recalling what those letters mean and choosing appropriate strategies can be arduous.

The second tool that I want to introduce and use to close out this chapter—and book—is explaining how to structure communication when addressing difficult behaviors. This is by no means a lesson on how to have difficult conversations; whole books are written on that topic. My intention in introducing Gervase Bushe's Experience Cube is to help leaders understand not only how to structure communication with others, but more importantly, how to construct an accurate self-narrative of what they are observing and feeling. Once you are able to correctly identify the data driving your actions, you will be well-positioned to have the difficult conversations that so many leaders need to learn to have.

The Ladder of Inference represents how people go from selecting data to taking actions. The actions they take are part of an experience that begins with selecting data to inform their action and will end with the response their action elicits. The initial data, the action, and the response are all observable, whereas the underlying thought processes are not. More importantly, this experience involves other people who are forming their own narratives based on the same data. Often the narrative they form will be different from our own, and that disparity is what leads to conflict, especially when they want to take two very different actions. Gervase Bushe's Experience Cube is a model for deconstructing the narrative and making all rungs on the ladder visible.

Bushe's model, though, is not about having difficult conversations; it is used for having learning conversations, which are often termed as difficult conversations because we want someone else to agree with the actions we have chosen. By engaging in the following process, the goal is to gain a common understanding of the disparate experiences and use that disparity to agree on mutually beneficial actions. The act of building consensus is in and of itself an act of learning, as you are receiving new information that challenges your current assumptions and will ultimately affirm, shift, or change the conclusions drawn and actions taken. The model for these conversations is the following:

1. NOTICING

   What are you observing? State this to the other party by saying, "I notice that..." This is an opportunity to confirm both parties are referencing the same data.

2. INTERPRETING

   How have you interpreted that data and what assumptions are you making? State this to the other party by saying, "I think this [your assumption]." This now makes the ladder visible, as we can better understand the underlying reasons for the preferred action.

3. ASSUMING

   How does this assumption make you feel? What physical reaction did it elicit? State this to the other party by saying, "This has caused me to feel / act ... [feeling or action that has been observed, or perhaps not observed, by the other party.]" This now provides context for your behavior and also demonstrates being accountable for that feeling.

4. ACTING

   What actions do you want to result from debriefing this experience? What are the specific behaviors that need to be affirmed, modified, or changed completely? State this to the other party by saying, "I want ... [behavior or action that will contribute to the overall outcome.]" The behavior or action you want may not be agreed to, but it at least clearly establishes an expectation from which a mutually beneficial understanding can be achieved.

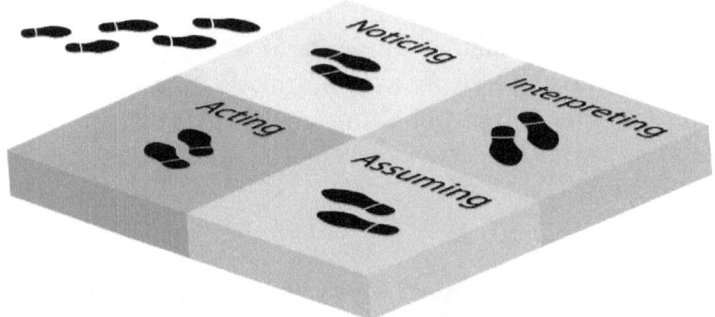

In Gervase Bushe's original article, he states that participants in this discussion should *Walk the Cube* as many as eight times. Walking the Cube in this case means structuring the discussion by Person A, in the first person, using "I" for each of the four steps, disclosing what they observed, the assumptions they made, how it made them feel, and the actions they sought or took as a result. Person B would then paraphrase what they heard, copying the same structure.

At this point, Bushe argues, it is important to understand how experiences are influenced in the moment; therefore, you need to walk the cube one more time for each person to explain how they feel in that moment. Person B would then commence sharing what they observed, the assumptions they made, how it made them feel, and the actions they sought or took as a result. Person A would then paraphrase what they heard and together, in turn, they would "debrief that moment" to make transparent how this experience of walking the cube is shaping the overall experience.

Unfortunately, this strategy can't be employed effectively without considerable buy-in from all parties, as well as each party having studied and practiced this model for communication. This is not an equation where you can plug in the details and the output will be mutual understanding with an agreement to tangible actions. Just like everything else in this book, this type of discussion begins with trust, is specific to a shared goal, and is part of the agreed team process, which takes us back to the Forming Stage. This conversation is easy to manipulate if there is not trust or buy-in to the process and desired output. In that case, the model for communication will simply serve as a channel for venting frustration. Why, then, would I tease you with this and not want you to use it directly?

First, becoming an effective leader is a long journey fraught with frustrations and failure in which there is no one workshop, degree, book, or tool that you can readily and consistently rely on to help see you through myriad dilemmas. Every situation is inherently unique, even though we might label it the same, such as a "difficult conversation." Therefore, every experience we have must be processed in a transparent manner, hence the cube.

Those who persevere and see through the frustrations and failure will take time to understand the experience and search out resources and support to help them understand how to better respond in future situations. Professional growth will be realized when a narrative is created that has a beginning (observations) and an ending (actions), which you can share with others, and which will be codified in your mind. In order to ensure we construct an effective narrative, we need to understand how to make sense of the experience we have had and how it can be used to inform us in future similar situations. For the purposes of this book and for those at the beginning of the leadership journey, this is probably the most powerful use of the Experience Cube: understanding how a narrative is constructed and ensuring you are aware of all the variables that are being processed through it.

Now that we understand how to narrate an experience to inform good decision-making, we are in a good position to lead others and help them understand their experiences. Ideally, everyone on the team is working towards the same purpose, in which case understanding the experiences each team member has will help to understand conflict as it evolves. As team leader, when we meet with team members and listen to their narrative, we can actively listen for each quadrant of the Experience Cube and paraphrase what we hear by processing it through the cube. Additionally, we may need clarification for each quadrant of the cube, in which case we will ask questions, like:

- NOTICING   - To help me understand how you have drawn this conclusion, tell me what else you observed or other information that you relied on.

- INTERPRETING - How did that observation or this piece of information affect your thinking?

- ASSUMING   - Can you describe how you felt while you were observing or referencing this information?

- ACTING   - What actions would you have preferred to have taken or seen others take?

This form of consultative communication now helps to ensure clarity and provide greater insight into how you can support your team members. Clarity, it is important to note, is one of the most highly desirable characteristics of an Effective Leader, cross-culturally. Therefore, by engaging in this process, you aren't only demonstrating effective communication skills, but also leadership skills. Over time, this process of thinking, speaking, and acting will become ingrained in your subconscious.

Reflexively applying this tool will ensure you take time to understand the context in which the situation is occurring and who the stakeholders are. Even though there may be several difficult conversations about how one team member doesn't trust another, you will have a greater appreciation for how each team member thinks, speaks, and behaves differently. Furthermore, you will be aware that the observable data you thought was relevant for past difficult conversations may not be so in future cases.

As we imagine all the different scenarios that could have led to Team Member A not trusting Team Member B, one thing holds true in every scenario: before you can move forward, you need to be willing to go back to the beginning. If your objective is to foster interdependency within the team or to pursue a transformative outcome, then you must be willing to stop what you are doing, work back through the stages of team development, and ensure all team members are clear on what it is the team is working toward and what their role is, acknowledging that only as a team can that outcome be achieved.

—FINAL THOUGHTS—

There is no playbook for achieving transformative change. What has worked for one team, or one school will not work exactly as it was implemented in its original environment in a new team or school. The work and experience we bring from other teams or schools can inform planning, but middle leaders must be able to make sense of the experiences they are having in that moment, including conflict and failure, so they can adapt and be successful in the environment where they seek change.

To achieve transformational change, there needs to be acceptance of conflict and failure. Conflict and failure are important tools to inform middle leaders of how the environment is responding to the actions being taken. They are an opportunity to pause, debrief, and adjust the course of action, even if it means starting over. Starting over may mean reassessing the very questions that should have been asked when identifying who should lead:

1. Does this candidate have the experience and interpersonal skills to foster a culture of interdependency within the team?
2. Does this candidate have the resources and relationships necessary to achieve the desired outcome?
3. Does this candidate have the same skills and attributes as other middle leaders who have successfully achieved similar outcomes?

No to any one of these questions does not imply someone is not fit to lead, but they should be the starting point for identifying how to professionally develop the middle leader.

Visit www.middleleader.com and subscribe to Michael Iannini's monthly Middle Leadership newsletter. Both the website and newsletter offer a variety of leadership development resources.

ENDNOTES

PREFACE

[1] PD as an acronym is used regularly throughout this book, particularly in Chapter 6, where the purpose and processes for training middle leaders are explored in depth. It is used as a title for coordinators and teams, as well as periods of time devoted to professional development. Anything related to training is commonly referred to as PD.

CHAPTER 2

[2] I use this acronym throughout the book. There are many types of professional learning communities and I do not subscribe to any one of them. I use this term in a general sense to refer to a group of teachers that have been assigned to a team to explore some area of practice.

CHAPTER 3

[3] Capacity-building is a term I use regularly in this book. That will be explored in detail in Chapter 6, as to how we can develop or build the capacity of middle leaders, to assume a larger role with greater responsibility to their team.

CHAPTER 4

[4] This will be discussed in greater detail when I introduce the Inference Ladder in Chapter 11 as a mechanism for team members to effectively harness disparity in perceptions to improve performance.

CHAPTER 5

[5] For the purpose of this case, I am using the British system for grade levels, which distinguishes age levels by the term year and not grade; year 1

is equivalent to the North American level of kindergarten, therefore there are 13 year levels.

CHAPTER 6

[6] Each stage is defined in Chapter 7.

[7] This list was also created to demonstrate to staff that PD included more than just external workshops or visiting consultants, so as to encourage them to take greater ownership of their professional development, which they often complained was limited by budget.

[8] These are often informal meetings between teachers from different schools, but who have the same or similar position, and share ideas or practices around a specific topic.

CHAPTER 9

[9] Dilts, R. (1994). *Effective presentation skills.* Capitola, CA: Meta.

[10] James C. Collins and Jerry I. Porras, *Building Your Company's Vision*, Harvard Business Review, September–October 1996.

[11] The other statements I have drafted personally and do not represent the school. As of the time of writing this book, I have not worked with the various teams in the school for a number of years. I also would not publish anything about a client that isn't already part of the public domain.

CHAPTER 10

[12] In Chapter 11, the Experience Cube is introduced as an activity to help team members develop the capability to be aware of their own thoughts and feelings during meetings, as well as how to become aware of and understand the thoughts and feelings of other team members.

CHAPTER 11

[13] The Ladder of Inference was first put forward by organizational psychologist Chris Argyris and used by Peter Senge in *The Fifth Discipline: The Art and Practice of the Learning Organization.*

BIOGRAPHY

Michael's journey in education began 23 years ago as a research assistant at the Arizona State University Child Development Laboratory, where he studied mixed age playgroups and conducted studies of how children retain and recall information. Since moving to China in 1999, Michael was first a teacher and then left the education field to start up and grow two successful information technology businesses. One of Michael's start-ups was in India, which helped him to learn to reflect on his successes in China and adapt them to building effective intercultural teams. During these years Michael learned how to satisfy the needs of a diverse group of stakeholders, develop cross-cultural leadership and communication skills, as well as continue his studies in Building Effective Teams and Strategic Planning. Michael returned to the education field in 2009 and began to work with a number of Not-for-Profit Organizations, International and Chinese Bilingual schools to develop curriculum, train teachers, and consult leadership on staff capacity building strategies, which has included a long and mutually beneficial relationship with ACAMIS and the Council of International Schools. Michael lives in Hong Kong with his wife Barbara and two children, Helena and Marco; the team that continues to transform his life for the better, every day.

www.ingramcontent.com/pod-product-compliance
Lightning Source LLC
Chambersburg PA
CBHW020416080526
44584CB00014B/1361